THE ROLE OF SOCIAL MEDIA IN ADOLESCENT DEVELOPMENT

EXPLORING ITS IMPACT ON SELF-ESTEEM AND INTERPERSONAL RELATIONSHIPS

DR. MINAKSHI BANSAL

This book is dedicated to all the adolescents navigating the complex digital landscapes of today's world. May you find the courage to embrace your unique identities, forge genuine connections, and support one another with kindness and understanding.

To the parents and educators who guide them, may this work offer you insights and tools to help the young individuals in your care flourish in both their real and virtual lives.

And to my own family, whose unwavering support and love have always been my anchor and inspiration. This journey would not have been the same without you.

ᑅᑅᑅ

Contents

Contents

Contents

Prayer

"Om Bhadram Karnebhih Shrinuyama Devah
Bhadram Pashyemakshabhiryajatrah
Sthirairangais Tushtuvamsastanubhih
Vyashema Devahitam Yadayuh
Svasti Na Indro Vriddhashravah
Svasti Nah Pusha Vishwavedah
Svasti Nastarkshyo Arishtanemih
Svasti No Brihaspatir Dadhatu
Om Shantih Shantih Shantih"

This mantra is a prayer for universal well-being, invoking the blessings of various deities for protection, health, and happiness. It emphasizes the importance of experiencing the auspicious through all senses and living a life aligned with divine purpose. The repetition of "Shantih" at the end signifies a deep desire for peace in the individual, the environment, and the universe at large. This mantra is often recited as a prayer for peace, prosperity, and the physical and spiritual well-being of all beings.

ᕀᕀᕀ

About The Author

Dr. Minakshi Bansal, born in the bustling metropolis of Delhi, India, has led a life steeped in artistry, scholarly pursuit, and an unwavering commitment to societal betterment. Following her marriage, she relocated to Ahmedabad, Gujarat, where she has since blossomed into a multifaceted beacon of inspiration for many. Dr. Minakshi is not only recognized as a gifted artist in the realm of Fine Arts but also as an esteemed author, a devoted social worker and a dedicated research scholar in Psychology. Her journey, marked by a profound dedication to elevating those around her, especially the downtrodden and underprivileged children of society, is a testament to her deep-seated belief in the transformative power of engagement and empathy.

From her earliest days, Minakshi was distinguished by an insatiable appetite for reading. Her literary universe was inhabited by characters and narratives that spanned ethical tales, motivational and inspirational stories, and the mythic parables imbued with life lessons. This voracious reading habit was not merely for personal edification but was driven by a desire to distill and disseminate the essence of these narratives to foster the development of students and peers alike. She was particularly captivated by the lives and teachings of historical figures and spiritual leaders such as Adi Shankaracharya, Swami Vivekananda, Dr. APJ Abdul Kalam, Mahamana Pandit Madan Mohan Malviya, Mahatma Gandhi, Sardar Vallabhai Patel, and Vinoba Bhave, among others. Their philosophies and life stories fueled her ambition to embody their ideals of resilience, selflessness, and relentless pursuit of knowledge.

Dr. Minakshi's academic and practical engagement with psychology has been equally noteworthy. As a research scholar, her focus has been on exploring the intricate tapestry of the human psyche, aiming to unlock the potential for psychological well-being and societal harmony. Her scholarly work is complemented by her active involvement in social work, where she employs her academic insights to make tangible differences in the lives of the underprivileged. Her endeavours in social work are characterized by an innovative approach that combines traditional wisdom with contemporary psychological practices to address the multifaceted challenges faced by these communities.

Her artistic talents, another facet of her diverse capabilities, are not merely a personal passion but also serve as a medium through which she communicates and connects with others. Her art, rich in symbolism and emotional depth, reflects her philosophical inquiries and social concerns, offering viewers a glimpse into the breadth of her intellect and the depth of her compassion.

In addition to her contributions to the arts and social sciences, Dr. Minakshi has embraced the healing arts of Pranic Healing, mastering the techniques developed by Master Choa Kok Sui. This practice, which focuses on the manipulation of Prana or life energy to heal the body and aura, has been both a personal journey of discovery and a means through which she extends her healing touch to others. Her proficiency in Pranic Healing is complemented by her advocacy and teaching of various forms of meditation aimed at rejuvenation, personal betterment, and the cultivation of harmony within individuals and communities alike.

Dr. Minakshi's life is a narrative of relentless pursuit, not just of personal achievement but of the upliftment and empowerment of society at large. Her diverse interests and talents—spanning the arts, literature, psychology, and the healing practices—converge on a singular path of service. She embodies the spirit of the luminaries who inspired her, channelling their legacy through her actions and teachings. Through her books, art, and social initiatives, she continues to inspire a new generation to embark on their own journeys of self-discovery, resilience, and altruism.

Her commitment to social betterment, particularly her focus on uplifting underprivileged children, reflects a deep understanding of the transformative potential of education and personal development. By integrating her knowledge of psychology, her artistic sensibilities, and her healing practices, Dr. Bansal has developed a holistic approach to social work that addresses both the immediate needs and the long-term well-being of the communities she serves.

As an author, Dr. Minakshi's writings offer a blend of inspirational insights, practical wisdom, and reflective contemplations drawn from her extensive reading and life experiences. Her books serve as a guide for those seeking to navigate the complexities of life with grace, resilience, and purpose. Through her narratives, she extends an invitation to her readers to explore the depths of their own potential and to contribute meaningfully to the collective well-being of society.

In Dr. Minakshi Bansal, we find a remarkable synthesis of the artist, the scholar, the healer, and the social activist. Her life's work stands as a beacon of hope and a source of inspiration for individuals seeking to make a difference in the world. Her story is a compelling reminder of the power of individual action, rooted in compassion and driven by a profound commitment to the betterment of humanity. Dr. Minakshi's legacy is not just in the tangible outcomes of her efforts but in the enduring spirit of inquiry, empathy, and service that she embodies.

ϷϷϷ

Preface

In this age of rapid technological advancement and cultural shifts, the impact of social media on our lives is a topic that has captivated the attention of researchers, psychologists, and educators alike. The focus of our exploration is particularly pointed toward one of the most vulnerable and impressionable demographics: adolescents. This preface seeks to set the stage for a comprehensive analysis of how these digital platforms are shaping the psychological landscape in which young people develop, grow, and interact with one another.

The journey through adolescence is marked by the search for identity, the desire for acceptance, and the cultivation of personal and social skills that will endure into adulthood. In previous generations, this passage was navigated through direct interactions, in school hallways and at community centers. Today, much of this exploration and interaction occurs in the digital realm. Social media platforms, which are omnipresent in the lives of most teenagers, offer unique opportunities for self-expression and connection but also pose unprecedented risks and challenges.

The pervasive influence of social media reshapes the way adolescents see themselves and others, influencing their self-esteem in profound ways. Every like, comment, and share has the potential to not only validate but also to diminish one's sense of self-worth. The immediate and often public feedback loop that these platforms provide can result in a heightened state of anxiety, impacting how young people perceive their place in the world.

Moreover, social media has transformed the nature of relationships. Friendships that once were developed through continuous personal interaction now often start and evolve in digital spaces. The subtleties of non-verbal communication, so crucial to understanding human emotions and intentions, are often lost, and the permanence and pervasiveness of online personas can both connect and isolate. Adolescents are navigating complex social dynamics under the watchful eyes of an online audience, managing online personas that may or may not align with their real-world selves.

As we delve into these themes, it is crucial to approach our discussion with a balanced perspective. While there are significant challenges associated with social media use, there are also undeniable benefits. For many adolescents, online platforms serve as venues for creative expression and social support. They can connect young people from diverse backgrounds to a larger community than is available in their physical environment, exposing them to broader ideas and opportunities.

Our analysis is drawn from a variety of sources, including psychological studies, surveys, and real-world observations, to construct a holistic view of the current landscape. By understanding the role of social media in shaping adolescent lives, educators, parents, and policymakers can better support young people in navigating these digital spaces safely and healthily.

This exploration is not just academic; it is imperative for the well-being of future generations. The conclusions drawn here aim to inform and guide thoughtful engagement with social media, emphasizing the development of critical media literacy skills among adolescents. Such skills are crucial in helping young people critically evaluate the information and interactions they encounter online, fostering a healthier digital environment.

As we reflect on these issues, we invite educators, parents, psychologists, and the adolescents themselves to engage in this ongoing conversation. It is only through collaborative efforts and shared understanding that we can hope to leverage the benefits of social media while mitigating its risks. Our goal is to empower young people to use these powerful tools not only to connect and communicate but also to enhance their own lives and the world around them.

Integral to this discourse is the presentation of strategies and interventions that can mitigate the negative impacts of social media while enhancing its positive aspects. The book discusses practical advice for parents and educators on fostering a healthy social media environment. It also offers recommendations for policy measures that can protect and empower adolescents navigating these digital platforms.

In writing this book, a comprehensive methodological approach was employed, incorporating both quantitative and qualitative research findings from the field. This robust approach ensures that the insights and recommendations are well-founded and evidence-based. Each chapter is meticulously referenced, allowing readers to trace the research that supports the discussions and to further explore the topics of interest.

As we conclude, the book not only summarizes the key findings but also looks forward to the future landscape of social media and its potential developments. It encourages ongoing dialogue among all stakeholders involved in shaping the digital experiences of adolescents, emphasizing the need for adaptability and proactive engagement in this continually evolving space.

It is my hope that this book will serve as a valuable resource, offering insights and strategies that can help navigate the complexities of raising and educating adolescents in a world where social media is omnipresent. Whether you are a parent, educator, policymaker, or researcher, may you find the information within these pages enlightening and empowering as we strive to support the healthy development of young people in an increasingly digital society.

Dr. Minakshi Bansal
Social Activist
Ahmedabad, Gujarat, Bharat

ppp

ONE

INTRODUCTION TO SOCIAL MEDIA AND ADOLESCENCE

The advent of social media has reshaped the way individuals communicate, share information, and form relationships. This transformation is particularly profound among adolescents, who are among the most active users of these platforms. As they navigate through critical developmental stages, the intersection of social media and adolescence presents unique challenges and opportunities that are crucial to understand.

Social media platforms like Facebook, Instagram, Twitter, and Snapchat offer adolescents new ways to connect with peers and express themselves. These digital environments provide a venue for young people to explore their identities, develop social skills, and gain acceptance among their peers. However, the impact of these interactions on adolescent development is complex and multifaceted, influencing everything from self-esteem to interpersonal relationships.

Adolescence is a pivotal period in psychological development. It is marked by significant physical, emotional, and social changes. During this time, individuals begin to step out of the shadow of their parents and seek greater independence. They form stronger social ties outside their family and experience heightened sensitivity to peer acceptance and rejection. This stage is also characterized by a burgeoning exploration of identity as adolescents try to understand who they are and where they fit in the world.

The role of social media in adolescence can be viewed through various psychological lenses, including Erik Erikson's stages of psychosocial development. According to Erikson, adolescence is dominated by the conflict between identity and role confusion. Social media provides a platform for experimenting with different personas and observing the reactions they elicit from peers, which can either help in resolving this conflict or exacerbate confusions about one's identity.

The constant connectivity offered by social media platforms also introduces a new dimension to adolescent social life. It allows for an almost perpetual engagement with peers, which can have both positive and negative effects. On the positive side, social media can enhance feelings of belonging and connectedness. Adolescents can find communities and groups that share similar interests and experiences, which can be particularly empowering for those who feel marginalized or isolated in their offline lives.

However, the impact of social media on self-esteem can be dual. While it can provide positive reinforcement and a sense of community, it can also lead to comparisons, jealousy, and a feeling of inadequacy. The curated images and lives presented on social media often set unrealistic standards that adolescents may strive to meet, leading to decreased self-esteem when these standards are unattainable. Moreover, the immediacy and permanency of social media can amplify the effects of negative interactions or cyberbullying, which can be devastating during a period when self-esteem is still developing.

Interpersonal relationships are also significantly affected by social media. The platforms can help maintain and strengthen relationships through constant communication and shared experiences. However, they can also alter the nature of interactions. Face-to-face communication provides immediate feedback through verbal cues and body language, which are crucial for developing empathy and deeper emotional connections. In contrast, digital interactions might lack these nuances, leading to miscommunications and a possible superficiality in relationships.

The influence of social media on adolescence is further complicated by the rapid pace of technological change and cultural shifts. New platforms and trends emerge regularly, each with its own norms and modes of interaction. Keeping up with these changes can be both exciting and overwhelming for adolescents, who must continually adapt their social strategies and behaviors.

As adolescents navigate through their formative years, social media serves as a tool that can profoundly influence their psychological development. It affects their self-esteem, shapes their interpersonal relationships, and plays a critical role in their search for identity. Understanding these influences is crucial for parents, educators, and policymakers who aim to support adolescents in managing their social media use in ways that foster positive development and well-being.

ϸϸϸ

TWO

THE PSYCHOLOGY OF ADOLESCENTS: DEVELOPMENTAL PERSPECTIVES

Adolescence is a critical developmental stage that encompasses various psychological transformations, laying the foundation for adult identity and behavior. This period of life is marked by intense physical, cognitive, and emotional changes that influence how young people interact with the world around them. Understanding the psychological underpinnings of adolescents provides valuable insights into their behaviors, particularly in how they engage with innovative platforms like social media.

One of the primary psychological features of adolescence is the development of advanced cognitive abilities through what Jean Piaget terms the formal operational stage. This stage introduces the capacity for abstract thinking, allowing adolescents to process complex concepts, understand hypothetical scenarios, and consider future possibilities. This cognitive transition is significant as it influences how adolescents perceive themselves and their surroundings, including their engagement with digital environments.

The development of a personal identity is perhaps the most significant psychological task during adolescence. Erik Erikson described this phase as one characterized by the crisis of identity versus role confusion. Adolescents actively explore various roles, beliefs, and behaviors as they seek to establish a coherent sense of self. Social media platforms serve as a fertile ground for this exploration, offering a space where young people can experiment with different aspects of their identity, witness diverse lifestyles and opinions, and receive instantaneous feedback on their own expressions.

Another critical aspect of adolescent psychology is the heightened emotional intensity and variability experienced during this period. Neuroscientific research suggests that the adolescent brain undergoes substantial developmental changes, particularly in the areas responsible for emotion regulation and decision-making. The limbic system, which is crucial for processing emotions, develops ahead of the prefrontal cortex, the center for decision-making and impulse control. This imbalance can lead to increased risk-taking behaviors, emotional instability, and conflicts, which are often played out and sometimes exacerbated on social media platforms.

Social relationships also undergo significant transformations during adolescence. As individuals strive for greater independence from their parents, peer relationships become increasingly important. Adolescents are particularly sensitive to peer influences and approval as they develop their social identities. The omnipresence of social media in the lives of young people amplifies these peer interactions, providing both opportunities for social connection and risks such as peer pressure and exclusion.

The quest for autonomy is another defining characteristic of this developmental stage. Adolescents' growing desire for independence can lead to conflicts with authority figures as they push against boundaries. Social media can act as a double-edged sword in this quest; it can offer a sense of independence and control over one's social interactions, but it can also place adolescents at risk of exposure to harmful content or behaviors as they navigate these digital spaces without sufficient adult guidance.

Moral development is also key during adolescence. Lawrence Kohlberg's stages of moral development suggest that as adolescents grow, they move from a morality imposed by consequences or rules to a higher level of morality guided by universal ethical principles. Social media can influence this development by exposing adolescents to a wide array of moral and ethical dilemmas and diverse perspectives, which can either reinforce or challenge their moral viewpoints.

In adolescence, the importance of self-concept and self-esteem cannot be overstated. The feedback that adolescents receive from their environment, including peers, family, and increasingly, social media, plays a critical role in shaping their self-perception. Positive interactions and reinforcement can bolster self-esteem, while negative experiences, such as cyberbullying or social comparison, can severely undermine it.

In summary, adolescence is a complex and dynamic period of psychological development characterized by significant changes in cognitive functions, emotional regulation, identity formation, social relationships, autonomy, and moral reasoning. The integration of social media into the daily lives of adolescents intersects with all these developmental aspects, influencing and being influenced by the psychological growth that occurs during these formative years. Understanding these interactions is crucial for supporting adolescents in navigating both their real and virtual environments effectively and healthily.

ᗝᗝᗝ

"In the world of social media, every notification is a
reminder that you're seen, but the depth of connection
often remains shallow. We scroll through highlights and
feel the weight of our ordinary moments, measuring our
daily lives against a polished feed. This digital landscape
can erode our sense of self, leaving us to wonder who we
are beyond the screen. It's important to remember that
true self-worth cannot be measured in likes and
comments. Let's strive to find balance and authenticity in
our digital interactions."

ᗐᗐᗐ

THREE

UNDERSTANDING SELF-ESTEEM: FOUNDATIONS AND THEORIES

Self-esteem, a critical psychological construct, is an individual's subjective evaluation of their own worth. This concept encompasses beliefs about oneself (for example, "I am competent" or "I am worthy") as well as emotional states such as triumph, despair, pride, and shame. The foundation of self-esteem is shaped by various psychological theories and has profound implications for behavior, motivation, and well-being. Understanding the foundations and theories behind self-esteem provides crucial insights into its role in human psychology, especially during the formative adolescent years.

The roots of self-esteem can be traced to several psychological perspectives, each offering unique insights into its development and impact. One of the earliest frameworks was introduced by William James, who emphasized the importance of success versus pretensions in self-esteem. According to James, self-esteem is derived from achieving what one thinks one should achieve, thus suggesting that personal capabilities and achievements are fundamental in evaluating self-worth.

Building on this, the sociometer theory proposed by Mark Leary suggests that self-esteem is an internal gauge that measures the extent to which an individual is accepted versus rejected by others. From this perspective, self-esteem serves a social purpose, acting as a barometer for relational value and belongingness. This theory underscores the significance of interpersonal relationships and social acceptance in the development of self-esteem, which is particularly pertinent in the context of social media where feedback and social comparison are rampant.

Nathaniel Branden, one of the most influential figures in the field of self-esteem research, identified six pillars of self-esteem: living consciously, self-acceptance, self-responsibility, self-assertiveness, living purposefully, and personal integrity. These pillars highlight the actions and practices that support healthy self-esteem, emphasizing the active role individuals play in developing and maintaining their self-esteem. Branden's approach is particularly useful in understanding how adolescents can foster a resilient sense of self amidst the challenges posed by their social environments, including digital interactions.

From a cognitive perspective, Albert Ellis and Aaron Beck have contributed significantly to understanding the relationship between thought patterns and self-esteem. Cognitive theories of self-esteem focus on how irrational beliefs and negative thought patterns can lead to low self-esteem. Ellis introduced the concept of unconditional self-acceptance, arguing that by challenging and changing irrational beliefs, individuals could develop a healthier, more robust self-esteem. Similarly, Beck's cognitive therapy aims to alter the negative thought patterns that lead to low self-esteem, suggesting that by modifying these patterns, individuals can enhance their perception of self-worth.

Another influential model is the self-complexity theory, which posits that self-esteem is buffered by the complexity of an individual's self-concept. According to this theory, having a multifaceted self-concept, where one's identity is defined by multiple and diverse aspects of the self, can protect against the negative impact of failure in any single aspect. For adolescents, who are actively exploring various roles and identities, cultivating a diverse self-concept can be particularly beneficial.

Self-determination theory (SDT) provides additional insight into the development of self-esteem, emphasizing the role of autonomy, competence, and relatedness. According to SDT, fulfilling these basic psychological needs is essential for developing intrinsic motivation, well-being, and high self-esteem. In the context of adolescence and social media, the need for autonomy and competence can be significantly shaped by online interactions, while the need for relatedness can be both met and thwarted through digital platforms.

The understanding of self-esteem is also enriched by cultural considerations. Collectivist societies, for example, might emphasize relational self-esteem more than individualistic societies, where self-esteem is often viewed through personal achievements and individual qualities. This cultural dimension is essential in globalized social media environments where diverse cultural values and norms intersect.

Self-esteem is a multifaceted psychological construct influenced by various theories and perspectives. Each theory provides a lens through which the development of self-esteem can be understood and addressed, especially in dynamic contexts such as adolescence and social media usage. For adolescents navigating their social and self-identity in an increasingly digital world, these theories offer vital frameworks for understanding the complexities of self-esteem and its implications for their overall psychological health and development. Understanding these theoretical foundations helps in designing interventions and supports that promote healthy self-esteem, critical for well-being and success in life.

ppp

FOUR

INTERPERSONAL RELATIONSHIPS: AN OVERVIEW

Interpersonal relationships are integral to human experience, influencing well-being, emotional health, and even physical health. These relationships encompass a range of interactions among people, whether familial, platonic, romantic, or professional. Understanding the dynamics of interpersonal relationships is crucial, as these connections significantly impact an individual's life journey, particularly during the developmental stage of adolescence.

At its core, the study of interpersonal relationships involves exploring how individuals connect with, respond to, and influence each other in various settings. This field of study draws from multiple disciplines, including psychology, sociology, communication studies, and anthropology, providing a comprehensive understanding of the social bonds humans form.

The foundation of interpersonal relationships is communication. Effective communication is essential for the development and maintenance of healthy relationships. It involves not only the verbal exchange of ideas but also non-verbal cues such as body language, facial expressions, and tone of voice. Miscommunications can lead to conflicts and misunderstandings, which are natural aspects of any relationship but require skills and effort to resolve. Adolescents, who are still developing these skills, often experiment with different forms of communication on social media, which can both simulate and distort traditional interpersonal dynamics due to its lack of non-verbal cues.

Trust is another cornerstone of healthy interpersonal relationships. It develops from consistent and reliable behavior and communication. Building trust allows for deeper emotional connections and provides a safe space for individuals to express themselves and share their vulnerabilities. In adolescence, trust plays a pivotal role as individuals begin to distance themselves from parental figures and rely more heavily on peer relationships. The digital context of social media can complicate trust, as the anonymity and distance it provides can sometimes shield dishonesty and deceit.

Respect is equally vital in maintaining positive interpersonal relationships. It involves acknowledging and appreciating differences in opinions, desires, and needs without judgment. Respect allows individuals to feel valued and understood, fostering a supportive and nurturing environment. For adolescents, learning to navigate respect within peer groups and social media settings is crucial, as they encounter diverse perspectives and behaviors.

Conflict is inevitable in relationships and can stem from differences in opinion, miscommunications, or perceived slights. How conflicts are managed can either strengthen or weaken relationships. Effective conflict resolution involves active listening, empathy, negotiation, and compromise—skills that adolescents are actively developing. Social media can amplify conflicts due to its public nature and the speed at which information spreads, which can escalate situations before they can be adequately managed.

Empathy is the ability to understand and share the feelings of another, a critical skill in forming strong interpersonal relationships. It allows individuals to connect on a deeper emotional level, promoting compassion and supportiveness. For adolescents, developing empathy is key to navigating social complexities both offline and online. Social media can serve as a platform for expressing and practicing empathy, though the lack of face-to-face interaction may sometimes limit the depth of empathetic exchanges.

Interdependence in relationships refers to the mutual reliance on each other to meet emotional and physical needs. Healthy relationships strike a balance where interdependence does not become coercive or one-sided. Adolescents learn to balance their growing need for independence with the benefits of interdependence, a process that can be complicated by the sometimes superficial and fleeting interactions on social media.

The role of social networks extends beyond immediate personal interactions. Friends, family, acquaintances, and even larger societal structures influence how relationships are formed and maintained. For adolescents, their social network can include both offline and online communities, each with its norms and expectations. Social media expands these networks far beyond traditional boundaries, offering opportunities for global connections and exposure to diverse social norms and cultures, which can profoundly shape an adolescent's understanding and management of relationships.

Interpersonal relationships are complex and multifaceted, shaped by communication, trust, respect, conflict management, empathy, and interdependence. Each of these elements plays a significant role in the quality and stability of relationships. For adolescents, who are in a critical stage of social development, understanding and navigating these factors in both real and virtual spaces is essential. The interplay between these foundational elements of relationships and the influence of social media is a critical area of study, particularly given the profound impact these dynamics have on adolescent development and well-being.

ᗰᗰᗰ

"As adolescents navigate the tricky waters of identity and acceptance, social media serves as both compass and map. Yet, this digital terrain is fraught with illusions, portraying mirages of perfection that are hard to distinguish from reality. It teaches young minds to curate life rather than live it, to edit moments until they fit into the confines of societal approval. However, amidst these challenges lie opportunities for genuine connection. We must guide our youth to use these tools for building bridges rather than walls."

ÞÞÞ

FIVE

HISTORICAL EVOLUTION OF SOCIAL MEDIA PLATFORMS

The landscape of social media has undergone significant transformations since its inception, evolving from basic online communication tools to complex platforms that shape global culture, politics, and individual behavior. Understanding the historical evolution of social media platforms not only provides insight into their technological advancements but also reflects broader societal changes, particularly as these platforms have become integral to the daily lives of billions, including adolescents.

The origins of social media can be traced back to the early days of the internet when the web was primarily used for information retrieval and limited communication. The late 1990s and early 2000s marked the advent of the first social media platforms. SixDegrees, launched in 1997, is often considered the first true social media site because it allowed users to create profiles and friend other users. Although SixDegrees was short-lived, it laid the groundwork for the social media networks that would follow.

The early 2000s saw the emergence of platforms that began shaping the internet's social landscape significantly. Friendster, launched in 2002, and MySpace, launched in 2003, were among the first to gain massive popularity. They introduced features that are now standard in social media, such as customizable profiles and the ability to connect with friends and share media. MySpace, in particular, became a cultural phenomenon, deeply influencing music and youth culture. It was here that many young users first experienced an online community that felt personal and vibrant.

In 2004, the launch of Facebook marked a significant turning point in social media history. Originally exclusive to Harvard students, it quickly expanded to other universities and eventually to the general public in 2006. Facebook introduced the News Feed, which revolutionized how content was consumed and shared on social platforms. It aggregated updates from one's network into a constantly updating timeline, creating a new way for users to interact with social media.

Simultaneously, the mid-2000s witnessed the rise of other platforms that diversified the social media landscape. LinkedIn (launched in 2003) targeted professionals looking to network, while YouTube (launched in 2005) changed the way video content was shared and consumed. Twitter, launched in 2006, introduced microblogging, where users could broadcast short messages, or tweets, to the world, fundamentally changing how news and real-time events were communicated.

The late 2000s and early 2010s saw social media platforms become truly mobile with the rise of smartphones. Instagram, launched in 2010, took advantage of the smartphone's camera to allow users to share photos and, later, videos, with a focus on aesthetics and visual storytelling. Snapchat, launched in 2011, introduced messages that disappeared after being viewed, appealing to younger users with its ephemeral nature and fun communication style.

The proliferation of these platforms highlighted their ability to not only connect people but also serve as powerful tools for marketing, activism, and personal expression. Each platform created unique ways of interacting, from Instagram's filters and stories to Twitter's hashtags and retweets. These features encouraged users to engage not just with their friends but with larger communities and movements, thus amplifying their social impact.

Moreover, the evolution of these platforms has been characterized by an increasing sophistication in how they handle data. Algorithms designed to personalize content delivery have profoundly impacted user engagement, keeping individuals glued to their feeds and influencing everything from political opinions to personal preferences.

In recent years, newer platforms and technologies have continued to evolve. TikTok, for instance, has emerged as a dominant force, particularly among Gen Z users, by leveraging short-form, highly engaging video content. The platform's algorithm is particularly adept at surfacing content that keeps users watching, demonstrating the ongoing refinement of personalization technologies.

The historical evolution of social media reflects broader changes in technology, culture, and society. Each phase of development has introduced new features and possibilities, from basic networking and communication to complex interactions that include video sharing, real-time broadcasting, and ephemeral content. For adolescents today, navigating this complex and ever-changing landscape is a fundamental part of daily life, influencing their social interactions, personal identity, and worldviews. As we look to the future, understanding this historical context helps us appreciate the profound impact social media has on global communication patterns and individual relationships.

ÞÞÞ

SIX

THE DIGITAL LANDSCAPE: SOCIAL MEDIA USAGE STATISTICS

The digital landscape today is predominantly shaped by social media, which has become an integral part of daily life for billions of people around the world. The statistics surrounding social media usage not only illustrate its prevalence but also provide insights into behavioral trends, cultural shifts, and technological advancements. Understanding these statistics is crucial for grasping the scope and impact of social media across different demographics, including adolescents who are among its most active users.

Globally, the number of social media users has seen an exponential increase over the past decade. As of recent estimates, there are over 4.5 billion social media users worldwide, which constitutes about 57% of the global population. This growth has been propelled by broader internet penetration and the ubiquity of smartphones, which have made social media accessible in even the most remote areas.

Facebook, despite facing scrutiny over privacy and misinformation issues, remains the most widely used social media platform with over 2.8 billion monthly active users. Its vast user base underscores its role as a social staple in many people's digital lives, serving as a platform for connecting with friends and family, sharing news and personal updates, and engaging with community and interest groups.

Instagram, known for its visual content, follows with over 1 billion active users. Its popularity, especially among teenagers and young adults, is driven by features like Stories, Reels, and a strong focus on aesthetics and visual narratives. Instagram has also become a critical platform for influencers and brands, leveraging its highly engaged user base for marketing and commercial purposes.

YouTube, as the leading video-sharing platform, boasts approximately 2 billion logged-in users monthly. It serves as a primary source of entertainment, information, and education for users of all ages. YouTube's expansive reach is evidenced by the fact that over 1 billion hours of videos are watched daily on the platform, highlighting its role in shaping public opinions and trends.

Twitter, with its focus on brevity and real-time communication, reports over 330 million active users. It is particularly influential in news dissemination and public discourse, providing a platform for political figures, celebrities, and everyday users to share their thoughts on global events instantly.

Snapchat and TikTok, newer to the social media scene, have captured the youth demographic with their innovative content formats—ephemeral content and short-form videos, respectively. TikTok, in particular, has experienced meteoric growth, with over 800 million active users worldwide, becoming a cultural phenomenon that significantly influences music, dance, and internet slang.

The penetration of social media varies significantly by region and is influenced by factors such as internet accessibility, economic development, and cultural attitudes towards technology. For instance, East Asia accounts for a substantial portion of social media usage, driven by high rates of technology adoption and the popularity of local platforms like WeChat and Line. Conversely, regions with lower internet penetration rates, such as parts of Africa, see slower social media growth, although the numbers are rapidly increasing with the expansion of mobile connectivity.

Age distribution on social media platforms reveals critical trends about user engagement. The majority of social media users are young, with a significant proportion between the ages of 18 and 34. This demographic is particularly appealing to advertisers due to their spending power and their receptivity to digital marketing. However, there has been a noticeable increase in social media usage among older adults, challenging the perception that social media is predominantly a young person's environment.

The impact of social media on daily life is profound. On average, people spend about 2.5 hours per day on social media platforms. This high level of engagement impacts various aspects of life, including social interactions, shopping behaviors, and the consumption of news and entertainment. For adolescents, social media is not just a tool for socialization but a significant part of their developmental experience, affecting their social skills, self-esteem, and worldviews.

Social media usage statistics paint a comprehensive picture of its role in modern society. These platforms have transcended their origins as mere digital spaces for socializing, evolving into powerful tools that influence almost every aspect of life—from personal relationships to global politics. As social media continues to evolve, understanding these dynamics becomes crucial for navigating the digital age, particularly for the younger generations who are growing up in an increasingly connected world.

ᗽᗽᗽ

"Social media has the power to connect us across continents, to weave networks of shared interests and forge unlikely friendships. For adolescents, these connections can be lifelines, portals to new ideas and cultures. Yet, the same platforms can become arenas of competition and comparison, where self-esteem battles against curated perfection. We must teach our young ones to navigate these digital spaces with critical thinking and self-compassion. Let them learn to celebrate individuality and find communities that uplift and support."

ppp

SEVEN

METHODOLOGY FOR STUDYING SOCIAL MEDIA'S IMPACT

Studying the impact of social media on individuals and society involves a complex interplay of methodologies that draw from various academic disciplines including psychology, sociology, communications, and data science. Given the pervasive influence and rapid evolution of social media, researchers employ a range of qualitative and quantitative methods to explore its effects, adapt to its changing nature, and understand its multifaceted impact.

The starting point for any comprehensive study on social media involves defining the specific dimensions of social media use to be examined. This might include aspects such as the amount of time spent on platforms, the types of interactions (passive vs. active), and the nature of the content consumed (informational vs. entertainment). Clear definitions help in precisely identifying what aspects of social media use are being studied and how they relate to the impacts being measured.

Quantitative Methods

One of the primary quantitative methods used in studying social media is survey research. Surveys can gather data from a large number of individuals quickly and cost-effectively. They typically measure various aspects of social media usage, such as frequency and duration, and correlate these with various psychological or social outcomes such as levels of anxiety, depression, or social isolation. For instance, surveys might ask respondents to report their social media habits and their feelings of well-being to identify any correlations between increased usage and decreased mental health.

Another quantitative approach involves experimental designs, where researchers manipulate the social media environment to observe the effects on behavior or attitude changes. This might involve controlling the amount of time participants use a specific platform or the type of content they are exposed to. Experiments, particularly randomized controlled trials, provide strong evidence of causality but can be challenging to implement due to ethical considerations and the need for controlled settings that accurately reflect real-life social media use.

Longitudinal studies are also vital as they track changes over time, helping to ascertain whether shifts in social media use are associated with long-term changes in psychological well-being or social relationships. These studies can provide insights into the effects of prolonged exposure to social media and are invaluable in understanding trends and long-term outcomes.

Qualitative Methods

In-depth interviews and focus groups are commonly used qualitative methods that provide deeper insight into the personal experiences and perceptions of social media users. These methods allow participants to discuss their thoughts in their own words, offering rich, detailed data that can reveal the nuances of social media's impact on individual lives. For example, interviews might explore how individuals feel social media influences their self-esteem or interpersonal relationships and uncover personal stories that quantitative data cannot.

Ethnographic research is another qualitative approach where researchers immerse themselves in the communities and cultures formed around social media. This method is particularly useful for understanding how social media shapes community norms, communication styles, and group dynamics. Ethnographers might join specific online communities, observing interactions and cultural norms to gain a comprehensive understanding of social media's social and cultural impact.

Digital and Computational Methods

The rise of digital and computational methods has transformed how researchers study social media. Big data analytics allows for the analysis of vast amounts of unstructured data generated by social media platforms, such as tweets, posts, and comments. Machine learning models can analyze these data to detect patterns and trends, such as the spread of misinformation or changes in public sentiment over time.

Network analysis is another powerful tool in the digital method toolkit, which examines how individuals are interconnected through social networks. This method can help researchers understand the structure of online communities, the role of influencers, and the dynamics of information flow within networks.

Ethical Considerations

Studying social media also involves navigating numerous ethical considerations. Privacy is a paramount concern, as researchers must ensure that data collection and analysis safeguard participants' confidentiality and integrity. Informed consent, data anonymization, and ethical data use are crucial components of any research methodology in this field.

The methodologies for studying the impact of social media are diverse and must be carefully selected based on the specific research questions and the aspects of social media use being examined. Each method has its strengths and limitations, and often, a mixed-methods approach is employed to provide both breadth and depth in understanding social media's complex influences. As social media continues to evolve, so too must the methodologies used to study it, adapting to new technologies and the changing ways in which people interact online.

ᐅᐅᐅ

EIGHT

The Positive Effects of Social Media on Adolescents

Social media often receives attention for its potential negative impacts, yet there are also significant positive effects, particularly for adolescents. During this pivotal developmental stage, social media can offer unique opportunities for learning, socialization, and personal growth. Understanding these positive aspects is crucial for parents, educators, and policymakers who aim to create a balanced perspective on social media usage among young people.

Enhancing Communication and Social Connections

One of the primary benefits of social media for adolescents is the enhancement of communication and social skills. Social media provides a platform where young people can interact with a much broader network than they would typically encounter in their immediate physical environment. This exposure can lead to improved communication skills and greater social confidence. For many adolescents, social media is a tool that helps bridge geographical divides, allowing them to maintain relationships with friends and family who are not nearby, including those they meet at camps, schools, or during travel.

Moreover, social media platforms can serve as important venues for adolescents who might struggle with shyness or social anxiety in face-to-face interactions. The digital environment offers a controlled space where they can engage at their own pace without the immediate pressures that in-person interactions can sometimes invoke. This aspect can be particularly empowering, providing a stepping stone to more confident communication in various settings.

Access to Information and Educational Content

Social media also plays a crucial role in education and learning. Platforms like YouTube, Twitter, and even Instagram offer vast amounts of educational content, ranging from science tutorials to language learning and coding classes. Adolescents can access diverse resources that may not be available in their local schooling system, enhancing their knowledge and skills in areas of personal interest.

Additionally, social media can support homework and learning through peer collaboration and sharing of educational materials. Study groups can easily be formed online, where students share insights, ask questions, and work on projects collaboratively. This accessibility to peer support and resources can enhance learning outcomes and encourage a culture of knowledge sharing and collective problem-solving.

Supporting Identity and Self-Expression

Adolescence is a critical period for identity development, and social media can play a positive role by offering a platform for self-expression and identity exploration. Young people can explore different facets of their identity, experimenting with how they present themselves and receive feedback in various forms. For those exploring creative pursuits like writing, music, or art, social media provides a public stage to share their work, gain audience feedback, and refine their skills.

Importantly, social media can be particularly valuable for adolescents who feel marginalized or isolated in their offline lives. For example, LGBTQ+ youth often find community and support through niche groups and forums that affirm their identity and experiences. These communities can offer essential support, reducing feelings of isolation and promoting a sense of belonging.

Fostering Civic Engagement and Global Awareness

Social media has the power to engage young people in civic and global issues. Platforms facilitate awareness and engagement with current events and social justice issues, providing a space for learning about and participating in civic matters. Adolescents use social media to organize, mobilize, and express their views on various issues, from climate change to human rights, which can cultivate a sense of agency and civic responsibility.

Moreover, the global nature of social media introduces adolescents to diverse cultures and perspectives, broadening their worldviews. This exposure can encourage empathy, cultural sensitivity, and a deeper understanding of global interconnectivity. It can also inspire activism and a desire to make a positive impact on the world.

Promoting Psychological Well-Being

While often scrutinized for its impact on mental health, social media can also promote psychological well-being by fostering a sense of community and belonging. For adolescents facing challenges or undergoing difficult experiences, social media can be a source of support and encouragement. Online support groups and forums provide spaces where young people can share their experiences, receive advice, and connect with others who have similar experiences.

The positive effects of social media on adolescents are significant and multifaceted. By enhancing communication, supporting education, fostering self-expression, encouraging civic engagement, and promoting well-being, social media can contribute positively to the developmental journey of young people. Recognizing and cultivating these positive aspects, while managing potential risks, is essential for helping adolescents navigate their social media experiences in healthy and productive ways.

ᑭᑭᑭ

"Every post and comment on social media carries the potential to influence, to harm or heal. Adolescents, in their formative years, are particularly vulnerable to these digital echoes. They are building their identities in a space where feedback is instant and often devoid of empathy. It's crucial that we instill in them the understanding that behind every screen is a human, deserving of respect and kindness. By fostering empathy and digital responsibility, we empower our youth to create a more compassionate online world."

❦❦❦

NINE

Negative Consequences of Social Media Use

While social media can offer various benefits, particularly for adolescents, it also presents a range of negative consequences. These impacts can affect mental health, social skills, and overall well-being. Understanding these drawbacks is essential for users, parents, educators, and policymakers to develop strategies to mitigate these effects and promote healthier social media use.

Impact on Mental Health

One of the most discussed negative aspects of social media is its impact on mental health. Studies and anecdotal evidence suggest that excessive social media use can lead to anxiety, depression, and feelings of inadequacy. This is often attributed to the "highlight reel" effect, where users compare their everyday lives to the idealized lives presented by others online. Adolescents, who are particularly vulnerable to peer approval, might feel that their own lives, appearances, or achievements are inadequate compared to those they see on social platforms.

Moreover, the need for likes, comments, and shares can lead to an obsession with social validation, which can erode self-esteem and increase stress. The instant nature of social media feedback can create a cycle where adolescents feel a constant pressure to post content that will receive approval, leading to an unhealthy focus on external validation rather than self-acceptance.

Cyberbullying and Online Harassment

Cyberbullying is another significant issue associated with social media. Unlike traditional bullying, cyberbullying can occur at any time and be relentless, as it is not limited to physical or temporal boundaries. Victims may feel like there is no escape from the harassment, which can lead to severe emotional distress. Cyberbullying can take various forms, including hateful comments, spreading rumors, and sharing private information without consent. Adolescents, who are still developing emotional resilience, can be particularly affected by these behaviors, which can lead to anxiety, depression, and in extreme cases, self-harm or suicidal thoughts.

Privacy Concerns and Data Security

Privacy issues are a critical concern in the realm of social media. Adolescents may not fully understand the implications of sharing personal information online, which can expose them to risks such as identity theft, stalking, or unwanted contact by strangers. Furthermore, the digital footprint left by online activities can be permanent, potentially affecting future opportunities and personal life. The sharing of content without consent, often seen in cases of "revenge porn," can have devastating effects on individuals, leading to emotional and psychological trauma.

Impact on Sleep and Physical Health

Excessive social media use can also negatively affect physical health, particularly concerning sleep patterns. Many adolescents stay up late, scrolling through social media, which can lead to sleep deprivation. Lack of sleep is associated with various health issues, including weakened immune function, reduced cognitive abilities, and poor academic performance. Additionally, the sedentary nature of prolonged social media use can contribute to obesity and related health problems.

Reduced Face-to-Face Interactions

While social media facilitates virtual connectivity, it can also reduce face-to-face social interactions. Real-life social skills, such as non-verbal cues and emotional empathy, are developed through direct interactions. Over-reliance on digital communication can hinder the development of these skills, leading to difficulties in personal and professional relationships. Adolescents may also experience a sense of loneliness and isolation, paradoxically feeling disconnected in an ever-connected world.

Distraction and Academic Performance

Social media can be a significant distraction, affecting students' focus and time management. The constant notifications and the allure of new content can interrupt studying and decrease productivity. This distraction can lead to poorer academic performance and reduced attention span, making it difficult for students to engage deeply with complex subjects or sustained tasks.

Shaping Worldviews and Perceptions

Social media platforms often use algorithms to tailor content to individual preferences, creating what is known as "echo chambers" or "filter bubbles." These bubbles can reinforce one's existing beliefs and limit exposure to diverse perspectives, potentially leading to radicalization or intolerance. For adolescents, who are still forming their worldviews, this can result in a skewed perception of reality, affecting their social and political understanding.

While social media has transformed how we connect and communicate, it is not without its pitfalls. The negative consequences associated with its use, particularly among adolescents, highlight the need for critical engagement and mindful usage of these platforms. By addressing these issues head-on, through education, parental guidance, and policy changes, we can help mitigate the adverse effects and foster a safer, more positive online environment for all users.

ԴԴԴ

TEN

Social Media and Identity Formation

Social media plays a pivotal role in identity formation, especially among adolescents, who are at a critical stage of developing their self-concept and sense of belonging in the world. The influence of social media on identity is profound and multifaceted, shaping how young people perceive themselves and others, navigate social norms, and express their individuality.

Exploration and Expression of Self

One of the fundamental ways social media impacts identity formation is through the opportunities it provides for self-exploration and expression. Platforms like Instagram, Snapchat, and TikTok allow adolescents to experiment with different facets of their identity through various types of content, such as photos, videos, and text posts. This virtual stage offers them a space to present themselves in ways that they perceive as ideal or aspirational. It also allows for feedback in the form of likes, comments, and shares, which can affirm or challenge their presentations and perceptions of self.

This process of identity experimentation is critical during adolescence, a time marked by Erik Erikson's psychosocial stage of identity vs. role confusion. Adolescents are actively seeking to understand who they are and how they fit into the world around them. Social media acts as a mirror reflecting a multitude of potential identities and social roles that can be tried on and adjusted based on peer reactions and internal reflections.

Influence of Peers and Media

The impact of peer interactions on social media is significant in shaping adolescents' identity. The immediate and often public feedback mechanism inherent in these platforms intensifies the influence peers have over an individual's self-image and behaviors. Positive reinforcement can enhance self-esteem and encourage further expression of certain traits or interests. Conversely, negative feedback can inhibit self-expression and even lead to changes in behavior to fit perceived social norms or expectations.

Moreover, social media exposes adolescents to a broader spectrum of cultural and social norms than they might encounter in their immediate physical environments. Through global connectivity, they can observe and interact with diverse groups, adopting styles, slang, behaviors, and viewpoints that transcend their local context. This exposure can significantly broaden their horizons, influencing their attitudes, beliefs, and self-perception.

The Role of Comparisons and Idealizations

Social comparison is another critical aspect of how social media influences identity formation. Platforms often encourage users to present idealized versions of their lives, leading to unrealistic benchmarks for personal success, beauty, and lifestyle. Adolescents, who are particularly sensitive to peer approval and social status, may feel pressured to conform to these idealized standards. This pressure can lead to feelings of inadequacy and low self-esteem when their real lives do not match the curated depictions they see online.

Cyberbullying and Its Impact

Identity formation can also be negatively impacted by cyberbullying, which is prevalent on many social media platforms. Being targeted by bullies can lead to a negative self-perception and a decrease in self-confidence. For some adolescents, the anonymity of online interactions emboldens them to explore negative aspects of their personality, which can become integrated into their identity. Victims of cyberbullying, on the other hand, might internalize the bullying and begin to see themselves in the terms used by their harassers.

Navigating Multiple Selves

A unique challenge posed by social media in the context of identity formation is the management of multiple online personas. Adolescents may present different versions of themselves on different platforms or even within the same platform, depending on the audience. Managing these varied personas can be complex and confusing, particularly when the boundaries between these online selves and their offline identity begin to blur.

Development of Autonomy and Agency

Despite these challenges, social media can also promote autonomy and agency, which are crucial components of identity formation. It provides a space where adolescents can make independent choices about how to present themselves, whom to interact with, and what interests to pursue. These decisions play a significant role in shaping their identity and sense of self-efficacy.

Long-term Implications

The long-term implications of social media on identity formation are still being studied, but it is clear that the influence is significant and lasting. As adolescents grow into adulthood, the identities they have shaped and solidified on social media often continue to influence their real-world choices and perceptions.

Social media is a powerful tool in the process of identity formation, offering both opportunities and challenges. It allows adolescents to explore and express their identities, connect with peers, and navigate social norms, but it also poses risks such as unrealistic comparisons, cyberbullying, and the stress of managing multiple online personas. Balancing these aspects is crucial for helping young people develop a healthy, coherent, and authentic sense of self in today's digital age.

ꝕꝕꝕ

"The paradox of social media lies in its ability to isolate us while promising connection. Adolescents can be surrounded by followers yet feel profoundly alone, their genuine struggles hidden behind a facade of filtered snapshots. This digital isolation can skew perceptions of normalcy and amplify feelings of inadequacy. We must encourage open conversations about the realities behind our screens. Promoting real-world interactions and authentic relationships can help mitigate the loneliness of the digital age."

ᛈᛈᛈ

ELEVEN

PEER INFLUENCE AND SOCIAL MEDIA INTERACTIONS

Social media serves as a critical arena for peer interactions, significantly influencing adolescents' behavior, attitudes, and personal development. This platform not only enhances the immediacy and breadth of peer influence but also changes the dynamics through which this influence is exerted. Understanding the depth and nuances of how peer influence operates in the social media context is crucial for comprehending its impact on young users.

Intensification of Peer Influence

The influence of peers during adolescence is well-documented in psychological research. This influence peaks during teenage years when individuals start to establish their identity outside of their family and look towards their peers for cues on social norms and behaviors. Social media amplifies this influence by providing a platform where peer interactions are not limited by physical presence or time. The constant connectivity means that adolescents are exposed to peer opinions and behaviors more frequently and intensely than ever before.

Social media allows for the display of likes, comments, and shares, which can serve as public endorsements or rejections of behaviors and opinions.

These metrics visibly quantify popularity and approval, powerful motivators for adolescents who are particularly sensitive to peer validation. As a result, the influence of peers on social media can directly shape behavior, encouraging conformity to what is perceived as popular or approved behavior within the peer group.

Echo Chambers and Reinforcement of Beliefs

Social media platforms typically use algorithms to tailor content that users see based on their previous interactions. This can lead to the creation of "echo chambers" where individuals are predominantly exposed to opinions and beliefs that reinforce their own. For adolescents, whose values and beliefs are still forming, this can significantly influence their development. If a teen is frequently exposed to a particular viewpoint or lifestyle that is echoed within their online community, they may adopt this perspective more readily, considering it normative and acceptable even if it is biased or polarized.

Social Learning and Modeling

Social learning theory, proposed by Albert Bandura, suggests that people learn within a social context, primarily through observation, imitation, and modeling. Social media serves as a potent environment for social learning, with peers constantly showcasing behaviors and outcomes that are either rewarded or punished. Adolescents observe these interactions and the reactions they garner, which informs their understanding of what behavior is appropriate or successful. This can include everything from lifestyle choices and fashion to political opinions and personal values.

For example, seeing peers engage in charitable activities and receive positive feedback for their actions on social media can encourage similar behavior in other adolescents. Conversely, observing peers engaging in risky behaviors and being praised or receiving attention for these actions might encourage imitation of such behaviors.

Cyberbullying and Peer Pressure

The darker side of peer influence on social media is manifested in cyberbullying and online peer pressure. Unlike traditional bullying, cyberbullying can be relentless and inescapable because it can occur at any time and in any place. This form of bullying can be particularly damaging as it is public and can rapidly reach a wide audience. The impact on the victim's self-esteem and mental health can be severe, as the bullying is not confined to an isolated incident but can be continuously accessible and sharable.

Peer pressure, similarly, is exacerbated on social media as adolescents feel compelled to conform to the group norms visible online, be it participating in certain online challenges, sharing similar opinions, or even engaging in risky behaviors. The need to belong and be accepted by peers can push adolescents to make choices they might not otherwise make in an offline setting.

Navigating Identity and Self-Esteem

Social media's role in identity formation and the influence of peer interactions therein can have profound effects on self-esteem. Adolescents are in the process of developing their self-concept, and the feedback they receive from peers via social media can significantly influence this self-perception. Positive reinforcement can boost self-esteem, while negative interactions or comparison with idealized portrayals of peers can lead to feelings of inadequacy and low self-esteem.

Peer influence on social media is a double-edged sword. While it can foster a sense of belonging and provide supportive community interactions, it can also lead to negative behaviors and attitudes through mechanisms like cyberbullying, echo chambers, and exacerbated peer pressure. The pervasiveness of social media in adolescents' lives means that peer influence is more significant than ever, necessitating a careful and nuanced understanding of how these dynamics work and how they can be managed to support healthy development. As we continue to navigate this ever-evolving digital landscape, it is crucial for parents, educators, and policymakers to create strategies that mitigate the negative aspects while enhancing the positive influences of peer interactions on social media.

ᐅᐅᐅ

TWELVE

The Role of Social Media in Friendship Dynamics

Social media has transformed the way friendships are formed, maintained, and sometimes ended. Its pervasive influence touches nearly every aspect of how individuals connect with one another, offering new opportunities and challenges that were unimaginable in the pre-digital era. The effects of these changes are particularly pronounced among adolescents, for whom social media is often a primary means of communication.

Formation of Friendships

One of the most significant impacts of social media on friendship dynamics is the way it has expanded the potential for making new friends. Platforms like Facebook, Instagram, and Twitter allow users to connect with people who share similar interests, values, or backgrounds, regardless of their geographical locations. This can be particularly beneficial for individuals who feel isolated in their physical environments due to unique hobbies, beliefs, or personal circumstances. For example, a teenager in a small town interested in niche activities like esports, rare literature genres, or specific music subcultures can find and connect with like-minded peers online.

Moreover, social media facilitates the initiation of friendships by lowering barriers to communication. Sending a message online can feel less daunting than approaching someone in person, which can encourage more frequent and open exchanges at the beginning of a friendship. This ease of interaction can accelerate the process of getting to know someone, allowing relationships to develop quicker than they might in face-to-face contexts.

Maintenance of Friendships

Social media also plays a crucial role in maintaining friendships. It provides various tools for friends to stay connected, share experiences, and support each other even when they cannot meet in person. Features like direct messaging, video calls, and status updates allow individuals to keep up with each other's lives, celebrating milestones or offering condolences despite physical distances.

Additionally, social media can help sustain friendships over time by providing a continual touchpoint for communication. Even minimal interactions, such as liking a photo or commenting on a post, can serve as reminders of a shared bond and maintain a sense of connection between friends. This can be particularly important for maintaining long-term relationships, which might otherwise fade without regular contact.

Changing Nature of Friendships

While social media can strengthen friendships, it can also change their nature. The volume of interactions that social media encourages can lead to more superficial relationships rather than deep, meaningful connections. The emphasis on public interactions, such as comments and likes, can sometimes prioritize quantity over quality, with friends feeling pressured to maintain an online presence instead of engaging in more substantive, private conversations.

Furthermore, the performative aspect of social media can affect how individuals present themselves to friends. The desire to appear successful, happy, or popular can lead to curated portrayals of one's life, which may not always reflect reality. This discrepancy between online personas and real life can create distances between friends, as they might feel they are connecting with a constructed image rather than a true friend.

Conflict and Misunderstandings

Social media can also be a breeding ground for conflicts and misunderstandings in friendships. Text-based communication lacks the non-verbal cues of face-to-face interactions, such as tone of voice and body language, which can lead to misinterpretations of intent or sentiment. A comment meant as a joke might be taken seriously, or a message meant to be supportive might be seen as patronizing.

Additionally, the public nature of many social media interactions can escalate conflicts. Disagreements that might have been resolved privately can become public spectacles, involving wider circles of friends or even strangers. This can complicate the resolution process and cause additional stress and embarrassment for those involved.

Digital Well-Being and Friendship

As the impact of social media on friendships becomes increasingly apparent, there is a growing focus on digital well-being. This involves being mindful of how online behaviors affect personal relationships and taking steps to foster healthy interactions. It can include setting boundaries around social media use, prioritizing face-to-face interactions, and being authentic in online communications.

Social media has deeply influenced friendship dynamics, offering new ways to connect and communicate while also presenting challenges that require careful navigation. As these platforms continue to evolve, understanding their role in friendship dynamics will be crucial for fostering healthy and supportive relationships in a digitally connected world.

ppp

"In the digital age, the challenge of adolescence is magnified; the quest for acceptance now plays out on a global stage. Social media can magnify insecurities but also offer a platform for self-expression and advocacy. It's a tool that, when used wisely, can amplify young voices and catalyze social change. We should guide our youth not just to navigate social media safely but to use it powerfully, to advocate for themselves and others. Encouraging responsible digital citizenship can turn online spaces into forums for positive growth."

❦❦❦

THIRTEEN

FAMILY DYNAMICS AND SOCIAL MEDIA ENGAGEMENT

The integration of social media into everyday life has profound implications for family dynamics, influencing communication patterns, relationship quality, and boundary-setting within families. As these platforms become ubiquitous, understanding their impact on family relationships is essential for fostering healthy interactions and mitigating potential conflicts.

Communication Patterns

Social media has revolutionized the way families communicate, both positively and negatively. On one hand, it facilitates connectivity, allowing family members to share life updates, photos, and messages instantly, regardless of geographic distance. This can be especially beneficial for extended families or those separated by circumstances such as migration or work commitments. For example, grandparents can follow their grandchildren's achievements and milestones via platforms like Facebook or Instagram, helping to maintain a bond despite physical separation.

On the other hand, the pervasive nature of social media can also disrupt traditional family communication patterns. The constant presence of mobile devices can lead to what is often termed 'technoference,' where the attention that might otherwise be directed towards family members is absorbed by digital interactions. This shift can diminish the quality of face-to-face interactions, with family members sitting together in the same room yet engaging more with their devices than with each other. The distraction posed by social media can lead to feelings of neglect or competition for attention, particularly among young children and teens who may feel less prioritized than their parents' digital activities.

Influence on Relationship Quality

The quality of familial relationships can be significantly influenced by social media use. Shared social media activities, such as playing online games together, participating in family group chats, or creating shared digital albums, can enhance relationship quality by building shared experiences and fostering a sense of closeness and belonging. However, when used excessively or inappropriately, social media can become a source of tension and conflict. Differences in opinions about appropriate content, privacy concerns, and the amount of time spent on social media can lead to disagreements and strain relationships.

Moreover, social media can expose family members to aspects of each other's lives that were previously private, leading to new dynamics of monitoring and surveillance. Parents might use social media to keep tabs on their children's social lives, which can lead to conflicts over privacy and autonomy, particularly with teenagers striving for independence. Similarly, children might gain insights into their parents' lives that can alter their perceptions or feelings, sometimes even stumbling upon information that parents might not have chosen to share directly with them.

Boundary Setting and Online Behavior

Navigating social media use requires careful boundary-setting within families. Each family must negotiate its own rules regarding social media engagement, such as deciding at what age children should be allowed on these platforms, setting limits on usage times, and determining what types of content are appropriate for sharing. These decisions can become contentious points within families, especially when there are differing views on the risks and benefits of social media use.

The process of setting these boundaries can also offer opportunities for teaching and learning. Parents have the chance to discuss important values such as respect, privacy, and empathy in the context of digital citizenship. By engaging in open discussions about social media use, families can address potential issues proactively, develop mutual understanding, and foster a responsible approach to digital engagement.

Social Media as a Tool for Family Cohesion

Despite the challenges, social media can also serve as a tool for family cohesion. During times of crisis or celebration, social media platforms can be powerful mediums for rallying support and maintaining connections. Families can use these tools to coordinate care, share important news, and provide emotional support to each other, regardless of physical location.

Furthermore, as family members navigate the complexities of social media together, they can strengthen their relationships through mutual support and guidance. For instance, parents can guide their children in developing healthy social media habits, while children can help parents navigate new technologies and platforms, creating a reciprocal learning environment.

Social media engagement significantly impacts family dynamics, influencing how family members interact, resolve conflicts, and support one another. While it presents new challenges and requires adjustments in communication patterns and boundary-setting, it also offers opportunities to enhance familial bonds and engagement. As families continue to navigate this digital terrain, finding a balance that preserves healthy relationships and embraces the benefits of social media will be crucial. Understanding and addressing the nuances of how social media affects family dynamics is key to harnessing its potential while minimizing its pitfalls.

⊳⊳⊳

FOURTEEN
SOCIAL COMPARISON AND SELF-ESTEEM

Social comparison, a theory originally formulated by psychologist Leon Festinger in 1954, posits that individuals have an innate drive to evaluate themselves, often in relation to others. This comparative process is profoundly influenced by social media, where the endless presentation of curated lives provides ample fodder for comparison. The impact of these comparisons on self-esteem is significant and complex, particularly as digital platforms become increasingly intertwined with daily life.

The Nature of Social Comparison

Social comparison on social media typically involves juxtaposing one's own life against the images and narratives presented by others. These comparisons can be upward, where individuals compare themselves to those they perceive as better off, or downward, where the comparison is with those deemed to be worse off. While upward comparisons can motivate and inspire, they more often lead to feelings of inadequacy and decreased self-esteem, especially when the benchmarks are perceived as unattainable. Conversely, downward comparisons might boost self-esteem temporarily, but they can also foster negative emotions such as complacency, guilt, or disdain.

Heightened Exposure to Idealized Realities

Social media platforms are replete with idealized portrayals that rarely reflect everyday reality. Users often present the best versions of their lives—highlighting success, beauty, and happiness while minimizing struggles and failures. This can create unrealistic standards that many find difficult, if not impossible, to meet. For adolescents and young adults, who are at critical stages of self-development, the constant exposure to such idealizations can distort their self-image and expectations, leading to dissatisfaction and low self-esteem.

The Impact on Self-Esteem

The relationship between social media use and self-esteem is a topic of considerable academic and social interest. Studies have indicated that prolonged exposure to idealized content on social media can lead to lower self-esteem. This is because frequent upward comparisons can diminish an individual's sense of self-worth and accomplishments. For example, seeing peers constantly posting about professional achievements, luxurious vacations, or perfect relationships can make individuals feel that their own lives are less successful or fulfilling.

Moreover, the quantitative aspects of social media, such as likes, comments, and shares, also play a crucial role in influencing self-esteem. These metrics often serve as tangible indicators of social approval and can significantly affect how individuals perceive their value and popularity. A lack of engagement with one's posts can be interpreted as a lack of social worth, leading to feelings of rejection and isolation.

Coping Mechanisms and Resilience

While the effects of social media on self-esteem can be challenging, individuals can develop coping mechanisms that help mitigate these impacts. One effective approach is developing an awareness of the curated nature of social media content, recognizing that it does not always represent reality. This awareness can help temper the effects of unfavorable comparisons.

Engaging in meaningful offline activities can also strengthen self-esteem. By investing time and energy in real-world interactions and achievements, individuals can build a sense of self-worth that is less dependent on online validation. Additionally, setting boundaries around social media use—such as designated times to log off—can help reduce exposure to harmful content and mitigate its psychological impacts.

The Role of Social Media Literacy

Educating individuals about the dynamics of social media is crucial in helping them navigate its challenges. Social media literacy programs that teach users about the psychological impacts of their online interactions can equip them with the tools needed to engage with these platforms in healthier ways. Such education can encourage critical thinking about the content one consumes and creates, promoting a more balanced and realistic engagement with social media.

The Importance of Support Systems

Strong support systems play a crucial role in buffering the negative effects of social comparison. Family and friends can provide essential perspectives and emotional support, helping individuals to contextualize their social media experiences within the broader scope of their real lives. Encouragement from trusted peers and family members can counterbalance the negative feedback or lack of engagement one might encounter online.

Social comparison facilitated by social media platforms can have profound impacts on self-esteem. These effects are particularly significant given the pervasive and integral role that social media plays in modern life. By understanding the mechanisms of social comparison and its effects on self-esteem, individuals can better navigate the challenges posed by digital environments. Developing healthy habits, enhancing social media literacy, and relying on robust support systems are all vital strategies for maintaining self-esteem in the age of ubiquitous digital presence.

ppp

"Navigating the highs and lows of social media is akin to sailing stormy seas. For adolescents, each like and comment can feel like a wave lifting them up or pulling them down. This tumultuous digital ocean can be overwhelming, but it also presents an opportunity to learn resilience. Teaching our youth to anchor themselves in the knowledge of their inherent worth helps them weather these storms. Let's equip them with the tools to sail confidently, maintaining their course amidst the ever-changing tides of social media."

ﬔﬔﬔ

FIFTEEN

Cyberbullying and Online Harassment

Cyberbullying and online harassment have emerged as significant issues in the digital age, especially with the increased use of social media. These behaviors involve the use of electronic communication to bully a person, typically by sending messages of an intimidating or threatening nature.

The impacts of cyberbullying can be devastating, affecting the mental health, self-esteem, and overall well-being of victims. Understanding the dynamics, effects, and preventive strategies associated with cyberbullying is crucial for protecting individuals and fostering a safe online environment.

The Nature of Cyberbullying

Cyberbullying can take various forms, including but not limited to, sending threatening or derogatory messages, spreading rumors online, sharing embarrassing or unauthorized photos or videos, and creating fake profiles to humiliate a person publicly. Unlike traditional bullying, cyberbullying does not require physical presence or strength and can occur at any time and place, which makes it particularly insidious and difficult to escape.

Perpetrators often exploit the anonymity afforded by the internet to harass their victims without immediate consequences, intensifying the sense of vulnerability among those targeted.

Scope and Impact

The scope of cyberbullying is vast, with individuals across all age groups at risk, though adolescents and young adults are particularly vulnerable due to their high engagement with digital communication platforms. The impacts of cyberbullying are profound; victims often experience a range of emotional responses including depression, anxiety, anger, and in severe cases, suicidal thoughts. The persistent nature of online content means that harmful messages and images can be difficult to erase, leading to prolonged distress.

Furthermore, the social nature of cyberbullying can lead to isolation and stigmatization from peers. Victims may withdraw from social interactions both online and offline to avoid harassment, leading to increased feelings of loneliness and social anxiety. The ripple effects can extend into their physical lives, affecting academic performance, personal relationships, and future job prospects.

Challenges in Addressing Cyberbullying

One of the primary challenges in addressing cyberbullying lies in its detection and the subsequent enforcement of consequences. Cyberbullies often hide behind pseudonyms or anonymous profiles, making it difficult to identify and punish them. Additionally, the global nature of the internet allows these behaviors to cross national boundaries, complicating legal actions due to differing laws regarding online harassment.

Another significant challenge is the reluctance of victims to report incidents, often due to fear of retaliation, embarrassment, or the belief that nothing can be done to help them. This underreporting contributes to the persistence of cyberbullying and can exacerbate the feeling of helplessness experienced by victims.

Preventive Measures and Strategies

Effective strategies to combat cyberbullying involve a combination of education, legal actions, and technological solutions. Educating individuals about the seriousness of cyberbullying and its consequences is fundamental. Schools, parents, and community organizations play critical roles in teaching young people about responsible online behavior and the importance of respecting others' dignity and privacy.

Legal measures are also vital in combating cyberbullying. Many countries have started to enact laws specifically targeting online harassment, giving victims and authorities the tools to take legal action against perpetrators. These laws also help to raise public awareness about the issue and affirm the commitment of societies to protect individuals from online abuse.

Technology companies and social media platforms have a responsibility to create safer online environments. This includes developing and implementing more effective algorithms to detect and block abusive content, providing users with robust tools to report harassment, and ensuring that reports are addressed promptly and effectively.

Partnerships between these companies, law enforcement, and mental health professionals can lead to more comprehensive approaches to prevent and respond to cyberbullying.

Support Systems and Rehabilitation

Support for victims is crucial for their recovery. Counseling services, support groups, and helplines can provide the necessary emotional support and practical advice to help victims cope with the effects of cyberbullying. Education on digital safety and privacy measures can also empower victims, potentially preventing future incidents.

For perpetrators, educational programs that focus on empathy training and the consequences of their actions are essential. Rehabilitation programs can help address the underlying issues that lead to such behavior, such as aggression, peer pressure, or a lack of attention at home.

Cyberbullying and online harassment are complex issues that require a multifaceted approach to effectively address. The collaboration of educators, parents, legal authorities, technology platforms, and the community at large is essential in creating a digital environment that is safe and respectful.

By understanding the dynamics of cyberbullying, its effects, and implementing proactive strategies, society can protect individuals from its harms and foster a culture of kindness and respect online.

ᐺᐺᐺ

SIXTEEN

THE IMPACT OF SOCIAL MEDIA ON MENTAL HEALTH

The widespread adoption of social media has significantly changed how people connect, communicate, and consume information. While it offers numerous benefits, such as enhanced communication and access to information, there is growing concern about its impact on mental health. This concern is particularly acute among adolescents and young adults, who are the most active users of these platforms. The effects of social media on mental health are complex and multifaceted, involving both positive and negative dimensions.

Connecting the Dots: Social Media Use and Psychological Effects

Social media platforms can serve as powerful tools for fostering connections and community. They allow users to maintain relationships with friends and family, join groups with similar interests, and participate in global conversations. For many, these interactions can provide emotional support, reduce feelings of isolation, and enhance a sense of belonging. However, the intensity and nature of online interactions can also lead to stress, anxiety, and depression. The mechanisms through which social media impacts mental health include social comparison, instant feedback, and constant connectivity, which can create a persistent sense of urgency and pressure.

Social Comparison and Its Discontents

One of the primary ways that social media can affect mental health is through the lens of social comparison. Users often encounter curated portrayals of others' lives, which can evoke feelings of envy, inadequacy, and lowered self-esteem. This phenomenon is particularly pronounced among teenagers and young adults, who are at a critical stage of developing their identities and self-esteem. Studies have shown that frequent exposure to idealized images of peers can lead to dissatisfaction with one's own life and achievements, which in turn can spiral into depression and anxiety.

Feedback Loops and Anxiety

The quest for likes, comments, and shares can lead to what psychologists refer to as 'contingent self-worth,' where individuals' self-esteem becomes overly dependent on the approval of others. This dependency can foster a state of chronic anxiety, as users constantly worry about how they are perceived online and whether their posts will be well-received. The immediate and public nature of this feedback can amplify feelings of anxiety, especially if the expected affirmations are not met.

The Paradox of Connectivity

While social media promotes a form of hyper-connectivity, allowing users to be constantly in touch with others, it can also lead to a sense of loneliness and isolation. This paradox arises because virtual interactions can sometimes replace more meaningful, face-to-face relationships.

The superficial connections fostered on social media might not provide the same emotional satisfaction and support that physical interactions offer, which can lead to feelings of loneliness and isolation, even as users are superficially more connected than ever before.

Impact on Sleep and Attention

The use of social media can also have indirect effects on mental health by disrupting sleep patterns and reducing attention spans. The blue light emitted by screens can interfere with the production of melatonin, the hormone that regulates sleep, leading to difficulties in falling asleep and poor sleep quality.

Additionally, the constant barrage of notifications and the habit of checking social media can fragment attention, making it harder for users to focus on tasks. This constant state of distraction can contribute to increased stress levels and reduced productivity, further impacting mental health.

Coping Mechanisms and Mitigation Strategies

Given the mixed effects of social media on mental health, it is crucial for users to develop effective coping strategies. These can include setting boundaries on social media use, such as designated 'unplugged' times or limiting notifications. Engaging in regular digital detoxes can also help mitigate the adverse effects of excessive social media use.

Additionally, cultivating awareness of the impacts of social media and actively choosing to engage in activities that promote mental well-being, such as physical exercise, meditation, and spending time in nature, can provide balance.

Role of Education and Awareness

Education plays a pivotal role in mitigating the negative impacts of social media on mental health. By raising awareness about the potential psychological effects and teaching healthy digital habits, individuals can be better equipped to navigate the challenges posed by these platforms. This education should start early, ideally in schools, where students can learn about the benefits and risks of social media use in a structured environment.

The relationship between social media and mental health is intricate and nuanced. While social media offers numerous opportunities for positive social engagement, it also presents significant challenges that can affect mental well-being.

Understanding these impacts is crucial for individuals, educators, and policymakers to develop strategies that leverage the benefits of social media while minimizing its potential harms. As the digital landscape continues to evolve, fostering a balanced approach to social media use will be essential for promoting overall mental health and well-being.

ϷϷϷ

"The digital footprint is a modern diary, unintentionally public and perilously permanent. Adolescents, with their future unfolding, must navigate the complexities of this online legacy. Social media requires them to make decisions that will linger far beyond their teenage years. Educating them about the long-term impacts of their digital choices is essential. By fostering awareness, we can help them build online identities that reflect their true selves and aspirations."

ᐁᐁᐁ

SEVENTEEN
Coping Mechanisms for Social Media Stress

In the digital age, social media has become an integral part of daily life for millions of people worldwide. While it offers unprecedented opportunities for connectivity and engagement, it also introduces unique sources of stress. These stressors can include information overload, social comparison, pressure to maintain an online presence, and exposure to cyberbullying. As such, developing effective coping mechanisms is essential for maintaining mental health and well-being in a hyper-connected world.

Understanding Social Media Stress

Social media stress often stems from the intense and constant engagement with digital platforms where users are bombarded with updates, notifications, and messages. This continuous stream can lead to feelings of being overwhelmed, a phenomenon sometimes referred to as 'digital fatigue.' Additionally, the culture of comparison facilitated by meticulously curated posts can make users feel inadequate or dissatisfied with their own lives. The stress of managing online personas and the fear of missing out (FOMO) can exacerbate feelings of anxiety and depression.

Strategies for Managing Social Media Stress

Set Boundaries and Limit Usage One of the most effective ways to manage social media stress is to set clear boundaries around its use. This can include designated times during the day when social media is avoided, such as during meals or right before bedtime. Many digital devices offer settings that help monitor and limit screen time, which can be utilized to keep social media use in check.

Cultivate Awareness Being aware of how social media usage impacts feelings and behavior is crucial. Users should check in with themselves to assess whether their social media interactions are mostly positive or if they leave them feeling sad, anxious, or upset. Awareness also involves recognizing signs of stress early and taking steps to address them before they escalate.

Engage in 'Digital Detoxes' Periodically disconnecting from digital devices, often referred to as a 'digital detox,' can provide much-needed relief from the constant pressure of online connectivity. This might involve taking a day or more off from social media each week or planning longer breaks during vacations or other significant times of rest.

Focus on Quality Over Quantity Reducing the number of social media platforms one uses can decrease the pressure to maintain multiple online personas. Focusing on fewer platforms or channels that bring the most joy or value can enhance the quality of online interactions and reduce the stress associated with managing numerous accounts.

Practice Mindful Engagement Practicing mindfulness while using social media can help mitigate the impact of negative content and reduce stress. This involves being fully present and consciously aware of one's experience while scrolling through feeds, actively choosing to engage with positive content, and avoiding comparisons.

Develop a Supportive Network Cultivating a network of supportive friends and family members on social media can buffer against stress. Engaging more with people who uplift and encourage rather than those who foster negativity can significantly enhance the quality of social media experiences.

Utilize Privacy Settings Understanding and using privacy settings on social media platforms can provide users with a sense of control over their online experiences. Controlling who sees one's information and posts can reduce the stress associated with unwanted interactions or the fear of being judged.

Seek Professional Help if Necessary When social media stress becomes overwhelming or contributes to anxiety or depression, seeking help from a mental health professional can be beneficial. Therapists can offer strategies to manage stress effectively and provide support in navigating digital challenges.

Foster Offline Relationships and Activities Ensuring that one's life offline is rich and fulfilling can lessen the impact of social media stress. Engaging in physical activities, pursuing hobbies, and spending time with loved ones in person can reinforce a healthy balance between the digital and real worlds.

Educate About Social Media Realities Understanding that much of what is seen on social media is curated and not an accurate reflection of real life can alleviate the pressure to measure up to unrealistic standards. Education about the nature of social media content can help individuals feel less isolated or inadequate about their own experiences and achievements.

Managing social media stress is crucial in today's digital landscape, where online interactions can significantly impact mental health. By implementing these coping strategies, individuals can enjoy the benefits of social media while minimizing its negative effects. Balancing online and offline life, setting boundaries, practicing mindfulness, and fostering real-world connections are all vital in building resilience against the stressors of social media.

ဧဧဧ

EIGHTEEN

PRIVACY, SAFETY, AND ETHICS IN SOCIAL MEDIA

Social media platforms serve as vital tools for communication, networking, and entertainment but also raise significant concerns related to privacy, safety, and ethics. As these platforms collect vast amounts of personal data and influence billions of lives globally, understanding the ethical considerations, privacy issues, and safety implications is crucial for users, developers, and policymakers.

Privacy Concerns on Social Media

Privacy is one of the most pressing concerns in the realm of social media. Users often share a wealth of personal information on these platforms, including details about their daily lives, personal thoughts, and location data. This information can be collected, stored, and analyzed by social media companies, often without explicit consent or clear understanding from users about how their data will be used or shared.

The commercial use of personal data for targeted advertising is one of the primary business models of free social platforms, which raises ethical questions about user consent and ownership of information.

Moreover, the data stored by social media platforms are vulnerable to breaches and misuse. There have been numerous instances where data leaks have exposed personal information to hackers and other malicious actors. Such breaches not only compromise personal privacy but also lead to potential financial fraud and identity theft.

Safety Issues

The safety of users on social media is another significant concern, particularly for vulnerable groups such as children and teenagers. Cyberbullying, grooming by predators, and exposure to harmful content are among the risks young users face when navigating these platforms. The anonymity and reach provided by social media can exacerbate these dangers, making it difficult to trace and prevent harmful behavior.

Social media platforms have been criticized for not doing enough to protect users from harmful content, including misinformation, hate speech, and extremist material. The rapid spread of false information can lead to real-world harm, as seen in various incidents of mob violence and the rise of health misinformation during the COVID-19 pandemic.

The challenge lies in balancing the need for open communication with the necessity to prevent the spread of harmful content, a dilemma that continues to provoke debate around censorship and freedom of speech.

Ethical Considerations

The ethical implications of social media use are vast and complex. Issues of content moderation, algorithm bias, and the psychological impact of platform designs are among the key concerns. Social media algorithms can create echo chambers that reinforce users' preexisting beliefs and isolate them from contrasting viewpoints, which can polarize public discourse.

Furthermore, the design of these platforms often emphasizes user engagement over quality of content, encouraging behaviors that maximize interaction (such as outrage or sensationalism) rather than informed discussion.

The ethics of social media also involve the responsibility of users in how they engage with others. The ease of spreading misinformation, engaging in slander, or violating others' privacy with few immediate repercussions raises questions about the ethical use of these powerful tools.

Strategies for Enhancing Privacy, Safety, and Ethics

Enhanced Privacy Controls Social media platforms need to provide users with robust privacy settings that are easy to understand and configure. This includes clear options to control who can see their information, how it is used, and whether it is shared with third parties.

Regular Audits and Transparency Reports Platforms should conduct regular audits of their data handling and security practices and publish transparency reports. These reports can help build trust by informing the public about the number of data requests from governments, the prevalence of harmful content, and the effectiveness of moderation efforts.

Ethical Design Principles Developing and implementing ethical design principles can mitigate some of the harmful psychological effects of social media. This might involve designing features that promote meaningful social interactions over superficial engagement metrics like likes and shares.

Education and Awareness Educating users about the safe and ethical use of social media is crucial. This includes understanding privacy settings, recognizing misinformation, and knowing how to report harmful content.

Regulation and Oversight Governments and regulatory bodies can play a role in ensuring that social media companies adhere to laws regarding privacy, data protection, and online safety. This might involve imposing fines for data breaches, mandating the removal of harmful content, and regulating the use of personal data for advertising.

Navigating the complexities of privacy, safety, and ethics in social media requires concerted efforts from various stakeholders including users, companies, and governments. By understanding and addressing these issues, the digital community can foster an environment where social media continues to serve as a tool for positive social engagement while minimizing potential harms.

This balanced approach is essential for the sustainable development of social media platforms and the protection of users' rights and well-being in the digital landscape.

ᐅᐅᐅ

"Social media's lens magnifies every success and every failure for teenagers, often distorting the scale of everyday life. This constant scrutiny can lead to pressure that is both intense and invisible. It's crucial that we help our youth understand that it's okay to step away, to recognize when social media becomes overwhelming. Encouraging them to seek spaces where they can be unfiltered and imperfect can foster a healthier relationship with their digital selves. Let's remind them that it's authenticity, not perfection, that truly connects us."

ᗺᗺᗺ

NINETEEN

GENDER DIFFERENCES IN SOCIAL MEDIA USE

The use of social media varies significantly across different demographics, with gender being a notable factor influencing how individuals engage with these platforms. Understanding gender differences in social media use is crucial not only for academic and marketing purposes but also for addressing issues related to online safety, mental health, and digital literacy. This essay delves into how gender affects social media preferences, behaviors, and experiences, shedding light on broader social dynamics and potential areas of concern.

Platform Preferences

One of the most apparent differences in how genders use social media concerns platform preference. Research indicates that women are more likely to use sites that emphasize social interactions, such as Facebook, Instagram, and Pinterest, which are platforms conducive to sharing and engaging with photos, personal experiences, and social updates. Men, on the other hand, tend to gravitate towards platforms like Twitter, Reddit, and LinkedIn, which are more oriented towards news, information sharing, and networking. These preferences reflect broader social trends where women engage more in social bonding and men in information seeking or status building.

Communication Styles and Content Sharing

Gender also influences communication styles on social media. Women are generally more expressive and tend to share more personal content, which includes updates about their lives and feelings. This style promotes engagement and interaction but can also expose women to higher risks of privacy breaches and cyberbullying. Men, conversely, often use social media for acquiring and sharing information rather than personal expression. Their interactions may be less frequent but involve more extensive networks, which can be advantageous for professional and informational gains.

Online Interactions and Community Building

Women are more likely to use social media to maintain relationships and build communities. They often participate in or moderate social groups that revolve around personal interests, family matters, or community issues. This use of social media as a tool for community engagement underscores the supportive nature of their online behaviors. Men's interactions, while less centered on community building, often involve more diverse networks, providing them with access to a broader range of opinions and topics, which can be beneficial for information gathering and diversity of thought.

Risk Exposure and Online Safety

The different ways men and women engage with social media also influence their exposure to online risks. Women are at a higher risk of sexual harassment, stalking, and contact by strangers, partly due to their higher engagement in personal sharing and community-building activities. These risks necessitate greater attention to privacy settings and online safety practices. Men, while generally experiencing lower levels of harassment, often face different types of online aggression, such as trolling and hate speech, particularly in politically or ideologically oriented spaces.

Mental Health Implications

The impact of social media on mental health also appears to vary by gender. Women are more likely to experience stress and anxiety related to social media, often due to social comparison and the pressure to maintain a certain image. The visual and interactive nature of platforms like Instagram and Facebook can exacerbate issues related to body image, self-esteem, and the perception of others' lives as superior. Men, while less affected by these particular issues, might experience stress related to the competitive aspects of social media, such as comparisons of success and status, particularly on platforms like LinkedIn.

Marketing and Consumer Behavior

From a marketing perspective, understanding gender differences in social media usage can help companies tailor their advertising and customer engagement strategies. Women tend to respond more to ads that foster a sense of community and provide value through tips, detailed explanations, or narratives. Men are often more receptive to ads that feature products or technologies and deliver quick, straightforward content.

Policy and Education

Recognizing these gender differences is essential for developing effective policies and educational programs that address the specific needs and concerns of different users. Educational initiatives can teach digital literacy and safety in ways that resonate with the distinct ways men and women use social media, improving their experiences and reducing potential harms.

Gender differences in social media use are marked and have significant implications for behavior, risk exposure, and mental health. By understanding and acknowledging these differences, users, platforms, and policymakers can create more inclusive, safe, and effective digital environments. This understanding also aids marketers in designing more targeted and effective campaigns that better align with the interests and behaviors of different gender groups, enhancing user engagement and satisfaction.

ᐯᐯᐯ

TWENTY
CULTURAL VARIATIONS IN SOCIAL MEDIA IMPACT

Social media has become a global phenomenon, but its effects are not uniform across different cultures. The impact of social media is shaped by a myriad of factors including national traditions, social norms, economic conditions, and regulatory environments, which vary significantly from one region to another. Understanding these cultural variations is essential for comprehending the broader implications of social media on global communication, behavior, and societal change.

Cultural Dimensions and Social Media Usage

Culture influences how individuals perceive and interact with the world, and by extension, how they use and respond to social media. Geert Hofstede's cultural dimensions theory provides a useful framework for understanding these differences. For example, in societies with high uncertainty avoidance, such as Japan and Greece, users might be more cautious about the information they share online and may prefer anonymous interactions.

Conversely, in cultures with low uncertainty avoidance like the United States and the United Kingdom, people may be more open to sharing personal information and engaging with strangers on social media.

Power distance, another of Hofstede's dimensions, can affect how individuals interact with authority figures on social media. In cultures with high power distance, such as Malaysia and the Philippines, there might be more hierarchical interactions on social media, where people are less likely to openly criticize authority figures.

In countries with low power distance, such as Denmark and New Zealand, social media might serve as a platform for more direct and democratic communication between citizens and their leaders.

Collectivism vs. Individualism

The collectivist versus individualist orientation of a culture also deeply impacts social media use. In collectivist societies like China and Mexico, social media usage is often more community-oriented with greater emphasis on maintaining group harmony and sharing content that benefits the group. Users in these cultures may prefer platforms that support group interactions and are more cautious about posting content that could disrupt social harmony.

In contrast, in individualistic cultures such as the United States and Australia, social media is often used as a platform for self-expression and individual identity. Users in these cultures may focus more on personal branding and the expression of individual opinions, which can lead to more diverse and sometimes confrontational content.

Regulation and Freedom of Expression

Cultural differences in the regulation of social media are significant and can affect how freely individuals can use these platforms. In some countries, social media is heavily censored and monitored by the government, as seen in China and Iran, where access to certain social media platforms is restricted, and content is closely monitored for political dissent or criticism.

In these environments, social media's role in public discourse is limited, and users may turn to coded language or other strategies to express forbidden views.

Conversely, in countries with more liberal attitudes toward freedom of expression, such as in Scandinavia, social media serves as a vibrant space for political debate, activism, and the free exchange of ideas. This openness can empower citizens and influence public policy but can also lead to challenges such as the spread of misinformation and the polarization of public opinion.

Social Norms and Online Behavior

Cultural norms regarding privacy, communication style, and interpersonal relationships also shape social media interactions. For instance, in Middle Eastern cultures, where personal relationships are highly valued and privacy concerns are significant, social media might be used differently, emphasizing strong personal connections and more private forms of communication.

In contrast, in Western cultures, where there is a higher tolerance for openness, users might be more willing to engage in public discussions and share personal details with a broad audience.

Adaptation and Innovation

Cultures also differ in their adaptation and innovation of social media. In South Korea and Japan, for example, local social media platforms like Line and KakaoTalk have been developed to meet specific cultural preferences for communication and privacy. These platforms offer features that are tailored to local users, such as digital stickers and characters that align with local communication styles, showing how cultural variations influence technological innovation.

The impact of social media varies widely across cultures, influenced by differing social norms, regulatory frameworks, and cultural values. These variations affect everything from the popularity of certain platforms within regions to the ways in which communities engage with technology and each other. Understanding these cultural distinctions is crucial for global companies operating in multiple countries, policymakers navigating international regulations, and individuals engaging in cross-cultural communication.

Recognizing and respecting these differences not only enriches the social media experience but also enhances the ability to harness these platforms for positive social, political, and economic impact on a global scale.

ॐॐॐ

"As adolescents scroll through endless feeds, the line between inspiration and intimidation can blur. The endless stream of achievements by peers can inspire but also pressure. It's important to teach young individuals that comparison can be a thief of joy, and that their value isn't determined by their productivity or visibility. Encouraging them to use social media to discover interests rather than validate worth can transform their experience from disheartening to enriching. Let us guide them to find joy in discovery and pride in personal progress, independent of online acclaim."

ppp

TWENTY-ONE

SOCIAL MEDIA AS A TOOL FOR EDUCATIONAL ENGAGEMENT

In recent years, social media has transcended its traditional role as a platform for social interaction and has emerged as a powerful tool for educational engagement. Its ability to facilitate communication, foster collaboration, and disseminate vast amounts of information has revolutionized the educational landscape. By tapping into the dynamic capabilities of social media, educators, students, and institutions can enhance learning experiences, expand educational access, and foster more profound engagement both inside and outside the classroom.

Enhancing Communication and Accessibility

One of the primary advantages of using social media in education is the enhancement of communication between educators and students. Platforms such as Twitter, Facebook, and LinkedIn allow for the quick dissemination of information, making it easier for teachers to make announcements, share resources, and provide feedback outside traditional classroom settings. This level of connectivity is particularly beneficial in creating a more inclusive educational environment that accommodates different learning styles and paces.

Moreover, social media breaks down geographical barriers, making education more accessible to students who might not have the resources or ability to attend traditional schools. For instance, students in remote areas can access lectures via YouTube, participate in real-time discussions through Twitter, or join study groups on Facebook. This accessibility not only democratizes education but also enriches it by incorporating diverse perspectives from around the globe.

Fostering Collaboration and Community Building

Social media naturally fosters collaboration and community building, which are crucial elements in modern education. Platforms like Slack and Discord have become popular in educational settings for facilitating group projects and discussions. These tools allow students to collaborate asynchronously, share files, and communicate effectively, regardless of their physical location.

Additionally, educators can create online communities that extend the learning experience beyond the classroom. For example, they might establish forums or Facebook groups where students can ask questions, share insights, and connect with peers who have similar academic interests. These communities not only support the academic development of students but also help in building networks that can be valuable for their future careers.

Integrating Multimedia and Interactive Content

Social media platforms are inherently multimedia, supporting text, images, videos, and interactive content. This versatility makes social media an excellent tool for creating and sharing educational materials that can cater to various learning preferences. Videos, infographics, podcasts, and interactive quizzes shared via social media can make learning more engaging and memorable.

Platforms like Instagram or Pinterest can be used to share visual content related to course materials, such as art, historical photos, or scientific diagrams, which can help students visualize complex information.

Similarly, Twitter's concise format is ideal for challenging students to express their thoughts clearly and concisely, a valuable skill in academic and professional settings.

Encouraging Real-Time Interaction and Feedback

Social media facilitates real-time interactions, which can be incredibly beneficial for educational purposes. Live-tweeting during lectures, using Facebook Live for classroom sessions, or creating Snapchat stories for field trips can engage students in unique and dynamic ways. These real-time interactions can also foster a sense of immediacy and relevance, making the educational content feel more connected to the real world.

Furthermore, the immediate feedback provided via social media can be highly motivating for students, as they can receive quick responses to their questions and posts. This feedback loop not only accelerates the learning process but also allows educators to gauge understanding and adjust their teaching strategies accordingly.

Professional Development and Lifelong Learning

Social media also serves as a platform for professional development and lifelong learning. Educators can join professional networks like LinkedIn to connect with peers, share resources, and stay updated on the latest educational trends and research. Professional learning networks across various social media platforms provide teachers with support and development opportunities that are essential for their growth and effectiveness.

Moreover, social media encourages lifelong learning by providing easy access to a vast array of educational resources. Adults looking to expand their knowledge or skills can follow educational pages, join specific interest groups, and access free courses and content shared through social media channels.

Social media offers diverse tools that can significantly enhance educational engagement. By leveraging its communication capabilities, collaborative nature, and multimedia support, educators can create more dynamic, inclusive, and effective educational environments. However, it is crucial to navigate the challenges such as distraction, misinformation, and the digital divide to maximize the benefits of social media in education. As educational practices continue to evolve, integrating social media in a balanced and thoughtful way will be key to enriching learning experiences and outcomes.

ppp

TWENTY-TWO

THE INFLUENCE OF INFLUENCERS: ROLE MODELS OR MISLEADERS?

The rise of social media has ushered in the era of the influencer, individuals who leverage their large online followings to shape opinions, behaviors, and even market trends. These influencers wield significant power, capable of reaching millions with a single post. However, with great power comes great responsibility, and the role of influencers in society is a double-edged sword. They can act as inspiring role models or misleading figures, and understanding the nuances of their influence is crucial for both consumers and the influencers themselves.

The Making of an Influencer

Influencers typically gain their status through a combination of charisma, expertise, and strategic use of social media platforms. They build their audiences by creating content that resonates with people's interests, desires, and needs. This content can range from fashion and beauty tips to fitness advice, lifestyle choices, and more serious topics such as mental health and political activism. Over time, influencers establish a sense of trust and authenticity with their followers, which is the bedrock of their influence.

Positive Influences: Role Models and Advocates

Many influencers use their platforms for positive impact, acting as role models and advocates for good causes. They can inspire change in lifestyles, encourage healthy habits, and motivate their followers to achieve personal goals. For instance, influencers in fitness and health promote exercise routines and nutritious diets, which can have a significant positive impact on public health.

In addition to lifestyle changes, influencers often champion social causes, from raising awareness about mental health issues to supporting charity initiatives. Their ability to reach a wide audience quickly and effectively makes them invaluable in disseminating important information and rallying support for good causes.

The Dark Side: Misinformation and Consumerism

However, the influence of influencers is not always benign. The pursuit of profit and popularity can sometimes lead influencers to engage in practices that are misleading or harmful. One of the most critical issues is the spread of misinformation. Influencers, often not experts in the fields they discuss, can disseminate inaccurate information to large audiences. This is particularly dangerous when it comes to health-related content, where misinformation can lead to serious consequences.

Furthermore, influencers often promote consumerism through sponsored content and endorsements. While advertising is a legitimate way to earn a living, excessive promotion, especially of unnecessary or harmful products, can perpetuate materialism and unrealistic lifestyles. The pressure to mimic the often-luxurious lifestyles portrayed by influencers can lead to financial imprudence among followers, particularly young people who are more impressionable.

Ethical Considerations and Transparency

Given their impact, it is crucial for influencers to operate ethically and transparently. This includes clearly disclosing partnerships and sponsorships, being honest about the benefits and limitations of the products or services they promote, and taking the time to research and understand the topics they discuss. Regulatory bodies in many countries are starting to enforce strict guidelines on these practices to ensure that influencers do not mislead their audiences.

The Role of Critical Media Literacy

For followers, developing critical media literacy is essential to navigate the complex landscape of influencer impact. This involves learning to question and critically assess the credibility of the content they consume on social media, understanding the commercial motivations behind certain posts, and recognizing their own susceptibility to persuasive techniques used by influencers.

Influencers can be both role models and misleaders, with the potential to inspire positive changes or foster harmful behaviors and attitudes. Their influence is a powerful tool that, if not handled responsibly, can lead to significant societal consequences. Both influencers and their audiences have roles to play in ensuring that this new form of social influence contributes positively to society. Influencers must adhere to high ethical standards, while followers must be vigilant and critical consumers of social media content. In this way, the digital landscape can remain a space for genuine inspiration and constructive engagement.

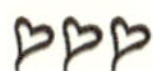

"Social media paints a complex portrait of modern adolescence, where every share and like is a brushstroke on the vast canvas of their developing identities. These platforms, while offering a space for expression, also demand a performance that can obscure authentic selves. It is vital for our youth to learn the art of discernment, to distinguish between the persona and the person. Encouraging them to connect offline as much as online can help balance their social experiences. Let's help them paint their stories with the vibrant colors of real life, not just the hues of digital approval."

ҎҎҎ

TWENTY-THREE

ADVERTISING AND CONSUMERISM THROUGH SOCIAL MEDIA

Social media has profoundly transformed advertising, creating new pathways for brands to engage with consumers directly and personally. This transformation has catalyzed a shift in consumer behavior and expanded the scope of consumerism in the digital age. Understanding how social media influences advertising and consumerism is crucial for marketers, consumers, and regulators alike, as they navigate the complexities of an increasingly digital marketplace.

The Mechanisms of Social Media Advertising

Social media platforms offer advertisers unparalleled access to large audiences along with sophisticated tools to target consumers based on a myriad of factors including interests, demographics, behavior, and more. This level of precision in targeting is unprecedented in the history of advertising and allows for highly customized advertising strategies. Platforms like Facebook, Instagram, Twitter, and Pinterest offer various formats for ads, from traditional banner ads to immersive video ads, sponsored posts, and interactive content.

The integration of e-commerce functionalities directly into social media platforms has further blurred the lines between advertising and direct sales. Features like Instagram's "Shop Now" buttons and Pinterest's "Buyable Pins" allow users to make purchases without ever leaving the platform, creating a seamless consumer experience from discovery to purchase.

The Impact on Consumer Behavior

The omnipresence of advertising on social media has significantly impacted consumer behavior. One of the most notable changes is the reduction in the decision-making process. Consumers are exposed to products and services immediately as they scroll through their feeds, often influenced by personalized ads tailored to their preferences and previous online activities. This immediacy can lead to impulse purchases and increased consumer spending.

Furthermore, social media has contributed to the rise of the "informed consumer." With easy access to reviews, product tutorials, and user testimonials all available on social media, consumers are better equipped to make informed decisions. However, this influx of information can also lead to analysis paralysis, where the overwhelming amount of data makes decision-making more difficult.

The Role of Influencers in Consumerism

Influencers play a pivotal role in shaping consumer preferences and trends through social media. Their endorsements of products or services can significantly sway their followers' purchasing decisions. This influence is so significant that many brands allocate substantial portions of their marketing budgets to influencer partnerships, recognizing the high return on investment that these collaborations can yield.

However, the reliance on influencer endorsements has raised concerns about consumer manipulation and the authenticity of influencer recommendations. The boundary between genuine preference and paid endorsement is often blurred, leading to potential mistrust among consumers. Regulators in many regions have begun to enforce strict guidelines requiring influencers to clearly disclose any financial relationships with brands to maintain transparency.

Consumerism and Cultural Shifts

Social media has also accelerated cultural shifts related to consumerism. The constant exposure to new products and the celebration of material wealth have heightened consumer desire for the latest and best items, perpetuating a culture of continuous consumption. This phenomenon is often criticized for promoting materialistic values and for its environmental impact, given the increased demand for fast fashion, electronic gadgets, and other consumables.

Addressing the Downsides

The adverse effects of heightened consumerism include not only increased material waste but also financial strain on individuals who feel pressured to keep up with trends. Additionally, the mental health implications of constant consumer pressure are significant, with studies linking materialism to reduced happiness and increased anxiety and depression.

Strategies for Mitigation

Consumers can mitigate these pressures by developing critical media literacy skills to discern the intent behind ads and to make more conscious purchasing decisions. Opting out of personalized advertising and actively managing social media usage can also reduce exposure to constant consumerist messaging.

For marketers, adopting ethical advertising practices that respect consumer intelligence and promote sustainable consumption is crucial. Brands that focus on quality and sustainability over mere volume of sales are likely to build stronger, more positive relationships with their customers.

Advertising through social media has reshaped the landscape of consumerism by changing how brands interact with consumers, influencing purchasing behaviors, and accelerating cultural shifts towards materialism. While social media offers numerous opportunities for brands to engage with audiences, it also presents challenges that require careful consideration of ethical, social, and psychological factors. For consumers, staying informed and mindful about the influence of social media on their purchasing decisions is key to navigating this complex landscape. Meanwhile, brands and marketers must balance their commercial objectives with ethical considerations to foster a healthier, more sustainable form of consumerism.

TWENTY-FOUR

SOCIAL MEDIA AND POLITICAL AWARENESS

Social media has emerged as a pivotal force in shaping political awareness and participation globally. It serves as both a platform for political expression and a catalyst for political movements, fundamentally altering the way citizens engage with politics and the democratic process. The role of social media in politics is complex and multifaceted, affecting everything from voter behavior to policy debates and the public's relationship with government.

Enhancing Political Engagement

Social media democratizes political communication by providing a platform where anyone can share their views, engage in political discussions, and mobilize support for causes. This accessibility has led to increased political engagement, particularly among younger demographics traditionally underrepresented in political processes. Platforms like Twitter, Facebook, and Instagram allow users to follow political leaders, advocacy groups, and news outlets, making it easier to stay informed and engaged with current events.

For many, social media serves as a primary source of news. It offers real-time updates on global events, often faster than traditional media outlets. The interactive nature of social media also allows users to discuss these events with peers, providing a more engaging and participatory form of news consumption. However, the reliance on social media for news also raises concerns about the accuracy and bias of the information consumed, as these platforms often lack the editorial standards of traditional media.

Mobilizing Social Movements

Social media has proven to be an effective tool for organizing and mobilizing social movements. The Arab Spring, Occupy Wall Street, and more recently, the global climate strikes illustrate how social media can facilitate the rapid organization and dissemination of protest activities. These platforms enable organizers to coordinate logistics, share strategies, and galvanize support, often bypassing state-controlled media and governmental restrictions.

The ability to create viral content also plays a crucial role in these movements. Hashtags become rallying cries that can draw global attention to local issues, transforming national movements into international causes. This virality can pressure governments and institutions to address the grievances being highlighted, demonstrating the power of networked individuals to influence political and social change.

Challenges of Misinformation and Polarization

While social media promotes political awareness and engagement, it also presents significant challenges. The spread of misinformation is perhaps the most critical issue. The same features that allow for rapid information sharing can also spread falsehoods and propaganda. During elections, for instance, the deliberate dissemination of false information can manipulate public opinion and influence electoral outcomes.

Moreover, the algorithmic nature of social media tends to create echo chambers, where users are predominantly exposed to viewpoints similar to their own. This effect can exacerbate political polarization, making it more challenging for individuals to understand opposing perspectives and reducing the possibility of consensus-building.

Influence on Policy and Governance

Social media impacts not just political awareness and campaigns but also policy and governance. Politicians and government agencies use social media to communicate directly with the public, bypassing traditional media channels. This direct communication can enhance transparency and accountability, but it also allows governments and political leaders to shape public discourse in unprecedented ways.

In democratic societies, social media can enhance government responsiveness, as leaders become more aware of public opinion on various issues. In authoritarian regimes, however, social media can be a double-edged sword: while it can offer a space for dissent, it can also be used by governments to surveil and repress opposition.

Strategies for Navigating Political Discourse on Social Media

Given the complex role of social media in political awareness, it is vital for users to navigate these platforms critically. Developing media literacy to distinguish between credible news sources and misinformation is crucial. Users should also seek out diverse perspectives to break out of echo chambers and gain a more holistic understanding of political issues.

For governments and policymakers, regulating social media without infringing on free speech remains a challenge. Policies aimed at increasing transparency about who is behind political ads and posts and what data is being collected can help mitigate some of the negative aspects of social media's influence on politics.

Social media has become an integral part of the political landscape, influencing how citizens engage with politics and how leaders govern. While it has undoubtedly enhanced political participation and awareness, it also presents significant challenges that require careful navigation. As society continues to grapple with these issues, the goal should be to harness the positive aspects of social media for political engagement while minimizing the risks associated with misinformation and polarization.

ϸϸϸ

"The silent pressure of constant connectivity can weigh heavily on young shoulders. Adolescents find themselves caught in a cycle of posting and monitoring for validation, their self-worth oscillating with their notifications. It is essential to teach them that their value does not diminish with their battery life. Encouraging periods of digital detox can help them reconnect with themselves and the tangible world around them. By fostering these habits, we support their mental health and help them establish boundaries that prioritize their well-being."

ppp

TWENTY-FIVE

THE LEGAL FRAMEWORK GOVERNING SOCIAL MEDIA

Social media platforms operate within complex legal frameworks that vary significantly across different jurisdictions. These laws and regulations are designed to address a range of issues, including user privacy, data protection, intellectual property rights, and content liability. As the influence of social media continues to expand, understanding the legal landscape in which these platforms operate is crucial for users, platform operators, and policymakers.

Data Protection and Privacy Laws

One of the most critical areas of legal concern for social media is the protection of personal data and user privacy. Laws such as the General Data Protection Regulation (GDPR) in the European Union have set high standards for privacy and data protection, granting users extensive rights over their data. Under GDPR, social media companies must ensure transparency about data collection processes, provide users with access to their data, and obtain explicit consent before collecting personal information. Users also have the right to request the deletion of their data under the "right to be forgotten."

In the United States, the legal framework for privacy is less comprehensive, with no equivalent to the GDPR at the federal level. However, specific states such as California have enacted laws like the California Consumer Privacy Act (CCPA), which offers privacy rights similar to those under GDPR. These laws require companies to disclose their data collection and sharing practices and provide users with the option to opt-out of data sharing.

Content Regulation and Censorship

Another significant legal issue is the regulation of content on social media. This includes laws addressing hate speech, misinformation, copyright infringement, and other forms of harmful content. The challenge lies in balancing the enforcement of these laws with the protection of free speech.

In many countries, social media platforms are legally obligated to remove illegal content once notified. However, the definition of what constitutes "illegal content" can vary widely between different jurisdictions. For example, hate speech is strictly regulated in Germany under the Network Enforcement Act, which requires platforms to remove illegal content within 24 hours of notification. Failure to comply can result in hefty fines.

In contrast, the United States protects speech to a greater extent under the First Amendment, including speech that may be considered hateful or offensive in other countries. Here, social media platforms generally are not held liable for user-generated content thanks to Section 230 of the Communications Decency Act, which grants platforms immunity from liability for the content their users post.

Intellectual Property Rights

Intellectual property rights are also a major concern in the realm of social media. These platforms host vast amounts of user-generated content, some of which may infringe on copyright or trademark rights. Social media companies must navigate complex intellectual property laws to determine when to remove content that potentially violates these rights.

The Digital Millennium Copyright Act (DMCA) in the U.S. provides a framework for copyright holders to request the takedown of infringing content. Social media platforms that comply with the DMCA's provisions are protected from copyright infringement liability. However, the process is often criticized for being prone to abuse by those who wish to suppress legitimate speech or competition through unjustified takedown notices.

Advertising and Consumer Protection Laws

Advertising on social media is another area heavily regulated by law. Advertisements must not be misleading or deceptive, and any sponsored content or endorsements must be clearly disclosed, according to laws enforced by agencies such as the Federal Trade Commission (FTC) in the U.S. Influencers and brands that fail to disclose promotional partnerships can face legal consequences.

Emerging Challenges and International Considerations

As social media continues to evolve, new legal challenges emerge. Issues such as the role of artificial intelligence in content moderation, the use of personal data for targeted advertising, and the impact of deepfakes are areas that current laws may not fully address.

Moreover, the global nature of social media complicates legal governance, as platforms must comply with the laws of all the countries where their users are located. This international aspect often leads to conflicts of law where platforms find themselves caught between complying with local regulations and adhering to their established policies and principles.

The legal framework governing social media is both vast and complex, reflecting the significant impact of these platforms on society. As social media evolves, so too must the laws and regulations that govern it, ensuring they protect users' rights and promote a healthy digital environment. For social media companies, navigating this legal landscape requires a careful balance between innovation and compliance, while for users, understanding these laws can empower them to use social media more safely and responsibly.

ppp

TWENTY-SIX

Psychological Theories Applied to Social Media Usage

The ubiquitous presence of social media in modern life invites a deeper psychological analysis to understand why and how people engage with these platforms so extensively. Several psychological theories provide a framework to explore the motivations behind social media usage, the effects on mental health and behavior, and the implications for identity and interpersonal relationships. Understanding these theories is crucial for users, psychologists, and developers to create healthier digital environments and improve individual well-being.

Social Cognitive Theory

Social cognitive theory, developed by Albert Bandura, emphasizes the role of observational learning, imitation, and modeling in learning new behaviors. Social media is a fertile ground for these processes, as users constantly observe others' behaviors and the resulting rewards. For instance, seeing someone receive positive feedback for a particular type of post (such as travel photos or fitness achievements) can encourage viewers to emulate this behavior, hoping to achieve similar social rewards. This theory helps explain trends and patterns in social media behavior, including how certain types of content become popular or why viral challenges spread so quickly.

Uses and Gratifications Theory

The uses and gratifications theory suggests that individuals actively choose media sources that satisfy specific needs and desires. Applied to social media, this theory proposes that users are drawn to platforms that meet various psychological needs such as social connection, entertainment, self-expression, and information seeking. For example, someone might use Facebook to fulfill a need for social interaction, while turning to Instagram for self-expression through photos and stories, or Twitter for real-time information. Understanding these motivations can help explain the diversity of social media use across different platforms.

Self-Determination Theory

Self-determination theory (SDT) focuses on the degree to which an individual's behavior is self-motivated and self-determined. In the context of social media, this theory can explain how the need for competence, autonomy, and relatedness drives engagement with these platforms. Social media can enhance feelings of competence through feedback mechanisms like likes and comments, satisfy the need for autonomy by allowing users to curate and control their online presence, and fulfill the need for relatedness through connections with others. However, if social media use is driven by external validation rather than intrinsic satisfaction, it can lead to psychological distress, showcasing the importance of autonomy in healthy social media use.

Cognitive Dissonance Theory

Cognitive dissonance theory, developed by Leon Festinger, is based on the premise that individuals experience discomfort (dissonance) arising from inconsistent beliefs, attitudes, or behaviors. Social media can exacerbate cognitive dissonance by continuously exposing users to idealized images and lifestyles that conflict with their reality or self-perception. For example, if a user believes they lead a fulfilling life but consistently sees posts from others depicting more glamorous lifestyles, this discrepancy can create dissonance. To reduce discomfort, users might change their perceptions or behaviors, such as by enhancing their online presence to appear more successful, which highlights the impact of social media on self-perception and mental health.

Attachment Theory

Attachment theory, originally developed to describe the dynamics of interpersonal relationships, can also be applied to understand interactions on social media. According to this theory, individuals form attachment styles early in life that influence their behavior in relationships. On social media, these styles can manifest in how individuals interact with others. For instance, someone with an anxious attachment style may seek constant reassurance through online interactions, while those with avoidant attachment styles may prefer limited and controlled interactions. Recognizing these patterns can help explain personal differences in social media engagement and the potential for social media to both soothe and exacerbate attachment-related anxieties.

These psychological theories provide valuable insights into the complex dynamics of social media usage. By applying these theories, researchers and practitioners can better understand the motivations behind social media behaviors, the effects on users' mental health, and the broader social implications. For users, gaining awareness of these psychological dynamics can lead to more mindful and self-aware engagement with social media platforms, potentially mitigating negative effects while enhancing the positive benefits. As social media continues to evolve, ongoing psychological research will be essential in adapting these theories to new technologies and changing social landscapes, ensuring that they remain relevant and beneficial in understanding and guiding social media use.

"In a world where adolescents can curate their lives with filters and captions, the distinction between reality and perception becomes blurred. Social media can craft a facade of flawless lives, silently escalating the expectations they place on themselves. It is our role to remind them that behind every perfect post is a real person with challenges and triumphs. Teaching them to approach social media with a critical eye can empower them to feel less isolated in their struggles. Let's guide them towards understanding and compassion for themselves and others."

ᐅᐅᐅ

TWENTY-SEVEN

QUANTITATIVE ANALYSIS OF SOCIAL MEDIA EFFECTS

Quantitative analysis plays a crucial role in understanding the multifaceted effects of social media on individual behavior, societal trends, and global communication. By applying statistical methods and data analysis techniques, researchers can uncover patterns, test hypotheses, and make predictions about the impact of social media. This approach provides empirical evidence that can inform policy decisions, guide corporate strategies, and enhance our understanding of digital interaction dynamics.

Data Collection in Social Media Research

The first step in quantitative analysis is data collection. Social media platforms generate vast amounts of data, including user demographics, engagement metrics (likes, comments, shares), time stamps, and content characteristics. Researchers often use APIs (Application Programming Interfaces) provided by platforms like Twitter, Facebook, and Instagram to collect this data systematically. Alternatively, surveys and experimental designs are employed to gather data on user perceptions, habits, and attitudes towards social media.

Statistical Methods and Analysis

Once data is collected, various statistical methods are applied to analyze it. Descriptive statistics provide a basic understanding of the data through measures like mean, median, mode, and standard deviation, helping to describe user behavior and content trends. Inferential statistics are used to make broader generalizations from the sample data to the larger population. This might involve hypothesis testing or regression analysis to explore relationships between variables, such as the impact of social media use on mental health.

Network Analysis

Network analysis is particularly relevant in social media research. It involves examining the relationships and structures within social networks to understand how information flows, how influential certain users are, and how communities form. Metrics such as betweenness centrality, closeness centrality, and degree centrality can reveal which users are central in spreading information or bridging different clusters within the network. This type of analysis is crucial for understanding phenomena like viral marketing, the spread of misinformation, or the dynamics of social movements.

Content Analysis

Quantitative content analysis involves coding and counting the occurrence of specific elements in social media content to analyze patterns over large datasets. For instance, researchers might quantify the frequency of specific words, hashtags, or themes to track trends or public sentiment. This method can be automated using software that applies natural language processing techniques to analyze text at scale. Content analysis helps in understanding the themes that dominate social media discussions, shifts in public opinion, and the prevalence of advertising content.

Time Series Analysis

Time series analysis examines data points collected or recorded at specific time intervals. In social media research, this method can help track changes in user engagement or sentiment over time. For example, analyzing tweet volumes and sentiments before, during, and after a political event can provide insights into how public opinion evolves in real time. This method is also used to assess the effectiveness of social media marketing campaigns or to monitor the rise and fall of viral phenomena.

Experimental and Quasi-Experimental Designs

Experimental designs, particularly randomized controlled trials, are often used to establish causal relationships. For example, researchers might use an experimental approach to determine if changes in the way social media feeds are organized affect user mood or satisfaction. Quasi-experimental designs, which lack random assignment, are also common when researchers need to study the effects of a natural intervention, such as the introduction of a new feature by a social media platform.

Ethical Considerations

Quantitative research in social media must navigate various ethical considerations. Issues such as user privacy, consent, and the potential misuse of data are paramount. Researchers must adhere to ethical guidelines that protect participants' anonymity and ensure that data collection and analysis do not harm the subjects of study.

Quantitative analysis provides a powerful toolkit for deciphering the complex effects of social media on modern society. Through rigorous data collection and sophisticated statistical methods, researchers can provide insights that not only deepen our understanding of digital social dynamics but also help mitigate potential harms and harness the positive potentials of social media. As social media continues to evolve, ongoing research and adaptation of quantitative methodologies will be essential in keeping pace with emerging trends and technologies.

༺༺༺

TWENTY-EIGHT

QUALITATIVE INSIGHTS FROM ADOLESCENT USERS

Qualitative research provides an in-depth understanding of human behavior, particularly valuable when exploring how adolescents interact with and are influenced by social media. This form of inquiry allows researchers to capture the nuanced emotions, experiences, and perspectives of young users, offering a rich tapestry of data that quantitative methods might overlook. By focusing on the voices of adolescents themselves, qualitative research sheds light on the complex interplay between social media usage and its impacts on their social, psychological, and emotional lives.

Methodologies in Qualitative Research

To gather qualitative insights, researchers employ various methods, such as interviews, focus groups, and ethnographic studies. In-depth, one-on-one interviews allow researchers to dive deep into individual experiences, exploring the nuanced ways adolescents engage with social media. Focus groups, on the other hand, provide a dynamic setting in which groups of adolescents can discuss their views and experiences, offering insights into social norms and peer influences. Ethnographic research, involving the observation of adolescents in their natural environments, helps researchers see how social media fits into their daily lives.

Themes in Adolescent Social Media Use

Identity Formation and Expression Adolescents are in a critical phase of identity development, and social media serves as a crucial platform for exploring and expressing their identities. Qualitative studies often reveal that social media allows young people to experiment with different aspects of their persona, from fashion and hobbies to political and social beliefs. This exploratory use can be empowering but also poses challenges as adolescents navigate the feedback and judgment they receive from their online peers.

Social Interaction and Belonging For many adolescents, social media is primarily a tool for maintaining and developing relationships. Qualitative research highlights how these platforms facilitate staying connected with friends, meeting new people with similar interests, and participating in online communities. However, the intensity and superficiality of some of these interactions can sometimes lead to feelings of loneliness and a sense of disconnection, suggesting a complex relationship between online interactions and real-life social satisfaction.

Peer Pressure and Social Comparison Adolescents are particularly sensitive to peer influence, and social media amplifies these pressures. Qualitative insights often reveal how constant exposure to peers' curated lives can lead to social comparison, affecting self-esteem and body image. Adolescents discuss the pressure to conform to perceived norms about appearance, success, and behavior, which can lead to anxiety and stress.

Learning and Information Access Many adolescents use social media as a tool for learning and information discovery. Through platforms like YouTube and educational blogs, they access tutorials, lectures, and other resources that support their educational pursuits. However, the challenge of distinguishing reliable from unreliable information is a significant concern highlighted in qualitative studies, pointing to the need for enhanced media literacy among young users.

Privacy Concerns and Risk Awareness Adolescents' understanding of privacy and risks associated with social media use is another area of interest in qualitative research. While some adolescents are highly aware and take steps to protect their privacy, others may not fully understand the implications of their online activities. Discussions around privacy settings, the permanence of online actions, and the potential for cyberbullying and exploitation are common in qualitative studies, indicating varied levels of awareness and concern among young users.

Empowerment and Advocacy Social media also serves as a platform for advocacy and empowerment among adolescents. Qualitative research captures stories of young people using social media to mobilize around causes they care about, from climate change to social justice. These activities not only contribute to a sense of agency but also help adolescents learn about civic engagement and the power of collective action.

Qualitative research offers invaluable insights into how adolescents experience and are influenced by social media. These insights highlight both the opportunities and challenges that these platforms present for young users. By understanding the nuanced perspectives of adolescents, parents, educators, and policymakers can better support them in navigating the complexities of social media use. This approach not only enhances the well-being of adolescents but also contributes to the development of healthier digital environments that respect and foster their growth and development.

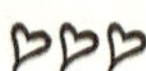

"The echo chamber of social media can amplify voices but also narrow perspectives, locking adolescents into feedback loops that reinforce their current views. Exposure to diverse ideas and opinions is crucial for their development into well-rounded individuals. We must encourage them to follow a variety of content, which can broaden their horizons and challenge their assumptions. By promoting digital literacy, we prepare them to navigate complex information landscapes. Let's help them build a foundation that values diversity and fosters growth."

ppp

TWENTY-NINE

CASE STUDIES: REAL-LIFE IMPACTS OF SOCIAL MEDIA

Social media has undeniably transformed modern life, influencing cultures, economies, personal relationships, and individual behaviors across the globe. The real-life impacts of these platforms can be observed through diverse case studies that demonstrate both the positive and negative effects of social media on individuals and communities. These case studies not only provide insight into the direct effects of social media but also help understand the complex web of interactions that define the digital age.

Case Study 1: The Arab Spring

One of the most significant political events influenced by social media was the Arab Spring, a series of anti-government protests and uprisings that spread across the Arab world in the early 2010s. Social media played a crucial role in organizing, mobilizing, and driving the protests that began in Tunisia in December 2010 and quickly spread to Egypt, Libya, Syria, and other countries.

Key Insights:

Mobilization: Activists used platforms like Facebook, Twitter, and YouTube to organize demonstrations, share ideas, and disseminate information on gathering spots and protest strategies.

Awareness and Exposure: Social media brought international attention to the human rights violations occurring in these countries, drawing global support and media coverage.

Government Response: The role of social media in these uprisings led several governments to temporarily shut down internet access or censor social media sites in an attempt to quell the protests.

Impact: The Arab Spring showcases social media's potential as a tool for political change, particularly in societies where free expression is suppressed. It highlighted how digital tools could empower citizens to challenge longstanding regimes and demand change.

Case Study 2: Cyberbullying and Mental Health

A contrasting case study is the story of Amanda Todd, a 15-year-old from Canada whose suicide in 2012 was attributed to severe cyberbullying. Amanda had shared a video on YouTube detailing her experiences with blackmail, harassment, and physical assaults, which were exacerbated by the relentless bullying she encountered online.

Key Insights:

Viral Nature of Harm: Social media can amplify personal traumas to a vast audience, increasing the psychological toll on victims.

Legal and Social Response: Amanda Todd's case led to a stronger call for laws addressing cyberbulic laws were enacted in several regions to prevent similar tragedies.

Impact: This case highlights the darker aspects of social media, including the potential for it to be a platform for harmful behaviors such as bullying and harassment. It underscores the urgent need for effective strategies to protect vulnerable users, especially adolescents, from online harm.

Case Study 3: Economic Opportunity through Social Media

On a positive note, social media has also created substantial economic opportunities for individuals and businesses. An example is the rise of Kylie Jenner, who used platforms like Instagram and Snapchat to build and promote her beauty empire, Kylie Cosmetics. By leveraging her massive social media following, she has become one of the youngest self-made billionaires.

Key Insights:

Marketing and Branding: Social media offers a powerful tool for personal branding and direct-to-consumer marketing.

Consumer Engagement: Interactive and personal content on social media helps in building customer loyalty and driving sales.

Influence and Reach: The case demonstrates how social media influencers can translate online popularity into substantial economic gain.

Impact: This case study illustrates the potential of social media as a platform for entrepreneurial ventures and economic growth. It shows how individuals can utilize digital platforms to launch successful businesses and achieve financial independence.

Case Study 4: Mental Health Awareness

Social media has also become a platform for raising awareness and reducing stigma around mental health. Celebrities and influencers, including Selena Gomez and Demi Lovato, have used their social media accounts to share personal stories about their struggles with mental health, encouraging others to seek help and support.

Key Insights:

Destigmatization: Open discussions about mental health on social media can help to break down stigmas.

Support Networks: Social media can foster supportive communities where individuals can share experiences and coping strategies.

Resource Sharing: Platforms can serve as valuable tools for spreading information about mental health resources and therapies.

Impact: These efforts on social media contribute to a broader understanding and normalization of mental health issues, making it easier for individuals to seek help without fear of judgment.

These case studies demonstrate the diverse impacts of social media on various aspects of life. From political revolutions and economic opportunities to the challenges of cyberbullying and the potential for mental health advocacy, social media continues to play a complex role in shaping modern society. By examining these real-life impacts, stakeholders can better strategize on harnessing the positive aspects of social media while mitigating its negative effects.

ᗰᗰᗰ

THIRTY

Technological Solutions for Safer Social Media Use

As social media becomes increasingly embedded in daily life, concerns about its safety and the well-being of its users have prompted the development of technological solutions aimed at creating a safer online environment. These innovations are crucial for protecting users from the myriad risks associated with social media, including cyberbullying, privacy breaches, misinformation, and unhealthy usage patterns. Exploring these technological solutions provides insights into how digital platforms can evolve to promote safety without compromising the benefits of connectivity and communication.

Advanced Moderation Tools

One of the primary challenges facing social media platforms is content moderation. Given the vast amount of content generated every second, manually monitoring all posts, comments, and interactions is impractical. Advanced moderation tools that use artificial intelligence (AI) and machine learning (ML) have been developed to address this issue.

These tools can automatically detect harmful content, such as hate speech, harassment, or explicit material, based on patterns and markers identified through training data.

For example, AI algorithms are trained to recognize text and image-based indicators of inappropriate content, allowing for real-time content filtering and removal. These systems can also learn from their interventions, adapting and improving their accuracy over time. However, the challenge remains to balance effective moderation with freedom of expression, ensuring that these tools do not inadvertently censor legitimate content.

Enhanced Privacy Protection Technologies

Privacy concerns are paramount among social media users, spurred by high-profile data breaches and unauthorized data sharing incidents. Technological solutions aimed at enhancing user privacy include end-to-end encryption, which ensures that messages can only be read by the sender and receiver, not even by the platform hosting the communication.

Blockchain technology also offers new avenues for protecting privacy. By decentralizing data storage, blockchain can potentially reduce the risk of mass data breaches. Additionally, it can provide users with more control over their data, allowing them to manage permissions and access through secure, transparent protocols.

Digital Well-being Tools

To combat issues related to social media addiction and its impact on mental health, platforms have started to introduce digital well-being tools. These features allow users to monitor their usage patterns and receive notifications when they exceed predetermined limits. For instance, apps like Instagram and Facebook have incorporated tools that track how much time a user spends on the app each day, providing weekly reports and reminders to take breaks.

Moreover, features like "Do Not Disturb" modes and notification silencers help users manage their online time more effectively, promoting healthier engagement with technology. These tools empower users to take control of their social media use, encouraging a more balanced online-offline life.

Real-time Assistance and Support Systems

Emerging technologies are also being used to provide real-time assistance and support to users who may be experiencing distress or who encounter harmful content. AI-powered chatbots can offer immediate psychological support and advice, directing users to professional help when necessary.

These bots can be programmed to recognize signs of distress or mental health crises in users' posts or messages, intervening with coping strategies or emergency contact information.

Misinformation Detection Systems

With the rise of 'fake news' and misinformation on social media, developing technological solutions to identify and flag unreliable content has become crucial. AI models are increasingly capable of analyzing news sources and rating their reliability based on previous outputs and known data about their accuracy. These systems can alert users to potentially false information before they share it, reducing the spread of misinformation.

Geolocation and User Verification Technologies

Improvements in geolocation services and user verification technologies also enhance social media safety. Geolocation can help in contextualizing posts and verifying the authenticity of content, which is particularly useful in emergency situations or disaster responses.

Meanwhile, advanced user verification processes, including biometric verification, can prevent unauthorized account access and reduce the risk of impersonation and fraud.

The development of technological solutions for safer social media use is an ongoing process that requires innovation, vigilance, and a proactive approach. As social media platforms continue to grow and evolve, so too must the technologies that ensure their safe use. By leveraging AI, blockchain, digital well-being tools, and other emerging technologies, it is possible to create a safer, more secure, and more supportive social media environment that enhances both individual and collective well-being.

These efforts are essential not only for protecting users but also for maintaining the integrity and sustainability of social media as a positive force in society.

ᐳᐳᐳ

"The instantaneous nature of social media can lead to impulsive decisions by young users, with repercussions that ripple far beyond the digital world. Teaching the importance of pausing to think before posting or reacting online can safeguard their reputations and their emotional health. Instilling the principles of thoughtfulness and responsibility in the digital age is essential. By emphasizing the permanence of the digital footprint, we can encourage more mindful interactions. Let's guide them to use social media not just as a platform for expression, but as a tool for thoughtful communication."

ᗡᗡᗡ

THIRTY-ONE

INTERVENTION STRATEGIES AND EDUCATIONAL PROGRAMS

In the context of addressing issues related to social media use, such as cyberbullying, misinformation, and digital addiction, intervention strategies and educational programs play crucial roles. These programs are designed to educate individuals about the responsible use of social media, enhance their ability to discern credible information, and develop skills to manage their online behavior healthily and effectively. By examining various strategies and programs that have been implemented across different settings, we can gain insights into what measures are effective in fostering a safer and more informed social media environment.

Educational Programs in Schools

Educational programs targeting social media use often start in schools, where children and adolescents first learn to navigate these platforms. Schools are pivotal in teaching digital citizenship, which encompasses a range of skills including ethical behavior online, understanding digital privacy, and recognizing online risks. For instance, programs that incorporate scenario-based learning can help students practice responding to situations like receiving a friend request from a stranger or encountering hostile messages. These educational interventions are designed to prepare students not just to protect themselves but also to engage positively in digital spaces.

Curricula may also include components on media literacy, which is crucial in helping students critically evaluate the content they encounter on social media. This includes distinguishing between facts and opinions, identifying biased reporting, and verifying sources. Media literacy programs aim to cultivate a skeptical and questioning approach to consuming information, which is essential in the age of digital misinformation.

Workshops for Parents and Guardians

As digital natives, many children and adolescents may navigate social media more intuitively than their parents. However, parents play a crucial role in guiding and monitoring their children's social media use. Workshops and seminars for parents can provide them with the knowledge and tools they need to support their children. These programs often cover topics such as the signs of cyberbullying, the implications of digital footprints, and strategies for setting reasonable boundaries around device use.

Parental education programs are most effective when they encourage open communication between parents and children about digital habits and experiences. This openness helps ensure that children can turn to their parents for help if they encounter problems online.

Community-Based Intervention Programs

Community centers, libraries, and non-profit organizations often host workshops and talks on safe social media use. These programs serve broader community members, including adults who may also face challenges such as digital harassment or privacy issues. Community-based programs are particularly important in reaching underserved populations who may have limited access to digital education resources.

For example, a community program might collaborate with local law enforcement to educate seniors about online scams and safe Internet practices. Another program might focus on helping immigrants and refugees use social media to connect with their families and access community resources safely.

Corporate Responsibility and Workplace Training

Companies, particularly those that operate social media platforms, have a responsibility to contribute to the safety and well-being of their users. Many tech companies have developed their own educational initiatives that promote safe and positive use of their platforms. These initiatives can include creating user guides, hosting live training sessions, and providing resources for mental health support.

Workplace training programs are also essential as they can address the professional aspects of social media use. These trainings often focus on maintaining professionalism online, understanding the impact of digital footprints on career prospects, and using corporate social media accounts responsibly.

Online Courses and Webinars

The accessibility of online education allows for widespread dissemination of learning resources related to social media use. Universities, tech companies, and educational websites offer courses and webinars that cover extensive topics from the basics of social media tools to advanced issues like data analytics and digital marketing strategies. These resources are invaluable for continuous learning and for keeping pace with rapidly evolving digital trends.

Monitoring and Evaluation

To ensure the effectiveness of these educational programs and intervention strategies, continuous monitoring and evaluation are necessary. Feedback mechanisms can be integrated into the programs to gather insights from participants and make necessary adjustments. Longitudinal studies and follow-up surveys can help assess the long-term impact of these interventions on participants' behavior and attitudes towards social media.

Intervention strategies and educational programs are vital in addressing the challenges posed by social media use. By educating various demographics—from young students to adults—and fostering a comprehensive understanding of digital environments, these programs play a critical role in shaping a safer, more informed, and responsible digital citizenry. As social media continues to evolve, so too must the strategies and programs designed to mitigate its risks and maximize its benefits.

ᐳᐳᐳ

THIRTY-TWO

PARENTAL GUIDANCE AND CONTROL MEASURES

As children and adolescents increasingly interact with the digital world, parental guidance and control measures have become crucial in ensuring a safe and positive experience online. Parents face the dual challenge of protecting their children from potential risks while fostering their ability to use technology responsibly. This responsibility involves not only applying control measures but also guiding children through the complex social, ethical, and safety issues associated with digital life.

Understanding the Digital Landscape

Effective parental guidance begins with a thorough understanding of the digital environment. This includes familiarity with various social media platforms, the types of content they host, and the common interactions they facilitate. Parents need to be aware of the potential risks associated with online activities, such as exposure to inappropriate content, cyberbullying, data privacy issues, and the risk of online predators.

Establishing Open Communication

The foundation of effective parental guidance is open communication between parents and children. This dialogue should encourage children to share their online experiences and concerns without fear of judgment or undue punishment. Establishing a routine for regular discussions about online activities can help parents stay informed about their child's digital life and provide timely advice or intervention if issues arise.

Setting Boundaries and Rules

Parents can set boundaries and rules that are appropriate for the child's age, maturity, and the specific risks they may face online. These rules might include:

Time limits: Setting specific times when children can use social media can help manage screen time and encourage a healthy balance between online activities and offline life.

Device-free zones: Establishing areas in the home where devices are not allowed, such as at the dinner table or in bedrooms at night, can encourage more family interaction and better sleep hygiene.

Privacy settings: Teaching children how to adjust privacy settings on social media accounts can protect them from unwanted contact and control who sees their posts.

Using Parental Control Tools

Technology offers a range of parental control tools that can assist in monitoring and managing a child's online behavior. These tools can:

Filter content: Blocking access to inappropriate websites and content based on age suitability.

Monitor usage: Providing reports on the amount of time spent on specific applications or websites.

Limit features: Restricting the ability to download apps, make in-app purchases, or use social media platforms unsuitable for their age group.

It's important for parents to explain the reason for implementing these controls, ensuring children understand that these measures are for their safety and well-being.

Educating About Online Safety

Education is a key component of parental guidance. Parents should educate their children about online safety practices, which include:

Personal information: Teaching children never to share personal information online, such as their address, phone number, or location without parental permission.

Recognizing threats: Helping children identify potentially dangerous situations online, such as requests from strangers or suspicious links, and knowing when to report these issues.

Social interactions: Discussing the implications of online interactions and the permanence of digital footprints, emphasizing the importance of kindness and the potential consequences of online behavior.

Modeling Appropriate Behavior

Children often emulate their parents' behavior, so it is crucial for parents to model appropriate digital behavior. This includes using devices responsibly, respecting others online, and maintaining a healthy balance between digital and real-life interactions.

Collaboration with Other Stakeholders

Parental efforts should be supported by collaboration with schools, communities, and even policymakers. Schools can support parental guidance through education programs and resources that teach children about digital literacy and safety. Communities can provide workshops or seminars for parents to learn more about digital parenting strategies.

Continuous Learning and Adaptation

Finally, the digital landscape is continuously evolving, requiring parents to stay informed about new platforms, trends, and potential risks. Engaging in continuous learning and seeking resources can help parents adapt their strategies as their children grow and as new technologies emerge.

Parental guidance and control measures are essential in safeguarding children's online experiences. By combining open communication, education, appropriate use of control tools, and modeling good behavior, parents can effectively guide their children through the complexities of the digital world. Collaborative efforts with schools and communities can enhance these initiatives, creating a comprehensive support system that fosters safe and responsible use of technology.

ᐅᐅᐅ

"Social media platforms, with their global reach and instantaneous feedback, can be arenas of immense psychological impact. For adolescents, this can mean unprecedented stress and anxiety. Providing a supportive environment where they can discuss their online experiences without judgment is crucial. We must offer strategies to handle online stress effectively, promoting resilience and a healthy mental state. Encouraging open dialogue about the emotional challenges of social media can demystify these experiences and provide needed support."

ᗡᗡᗡ

THIRTY-THREE

THE FUTURE OF SOCIAL MEDIA: TRENDS AND PREDICTIONS

As we look toward the future of social media, it is clear that the landscape is poised for continual transformation, driven by technological advancements, evolving user preferences, and shifts in cultural and regulatory frameworks. Understanding potential trends and making informed predictions about the future of these platforms can help businesses, policymakers, and users navigate the upcoming changes effectively.

Integration of Augmented and Virtual Reality

One of the most anticipated developments in social media involves the integration of augmented reality (AR) and virtual reality (VR). These technologies promise to revolutionize user interaction by creating more immersive and engaging experiences. For instance, AR can overlay digital information onto the physical world in real-time, enhancing the way users can share and interact with content. VR offers even more immersive possibilities, allowing users to enter entirely digital environments, which could redefine the concept of social presence and community. Platforms like Facebook are already exploring these technologies through projects like

Oculus and Horizon, aiming to create fully immersive social experiences.

Advancements in Artificial Intelligence

Artificial intelligence (AI) is set to play an increasingly central role in social media evolution. AI technologies can drive improvements in content personalization, ensuring that users see more of what interests them, thereby increasing engagement and time spent on platforms. AI is also crucial for moderating content at scale, identifying and removing inappropriate content before it reaches a broad audience. Furthermore, AI can enhance user analytics, providing more precise insights into user behavior and enabling more effective targeted advertising and content delivery.

Evolving Content Formats

The types of content that dominate social media are also expected to evolve. The recent surge in the popularity of short-form videos, exemplified by TikTok, suggests that dynamic and easily consumable content formats will continue to rise. Additionally, the growing interest in podcasts and live streaming points to an increased demand for more authentic and unedited content, which allows for deeper audience engagement and can build stronger personal connections between creators and viewers.

Decentralization and the Rise of Niche Platforms

As users become more concerned about privacy and data security, there is a potential shift towards decentralized social media platforms that prioritize user control over personal data. Blockchain technology could facilitate this shift, allowing for the creation of platforms where data is distributed across a network rather than stored on central servers. Simultaneously, the saturation of major platforms and the desire for more tailored social media experiences may lead to the rise of niche platforms that cater to specific interests, professions, or demographic groups.

Increased Regulatory Scrutiny

The regulatory landscape for social media is expected to become more stringent in response to growing concerns about privacy, misinformation, and the psychological impacts of platform algorithms. Governments worldwide are likely to introduce more comprehensive regulations that could reshape platform operations. For example, rules around data usage, content moderation, and algorithm transparency could significantly influence how platforms design their systems and manage user data.

Social Media for Social Good

There is an increasing expectation for social media platforms to contribute positively to society. This involves not only minimizing harm but also actively fostering beneficial outcomes. Platforms may increasingly be used to promote mental health awareness, support educational initiatives, and mobilize action on global issues like climate change and human rights. The potential for social media to serve as a tool for societal improvement is vast, provided that platforms can address the inherent challenges of ensuring these tools are used ethically and effectively.

Privacy-Focused Communication

In response to privacy concerns, there is likely to be a continued trend towards more private modes of communication. Features like ephemeral content, which disappears after a short period, and encrypted messaging, are likely to become more popular as users seek more control over their digital footprints.

The future of social media is marked by both challenges and opportunities. Technological advancements such as AR, VR, and AI are set to redefine user interactions, while shifts towards greater privacy, decentralization, and regulatory oversight will shape how platforms operate. As social media continues to evolve, it remains a powerful tool capable of influencing virtually every aspect of society. By anticipating these changes, stakeholders can prepare to leverage the benefits of social media while mitigating its risks, ensuring that its development continues to enhance human connectivity and community globally.

פפפ

THIRTY-FOUR

DEVELOPING HEALTHY SOCIAL MEDIA HABITS

In a world increasingly dominated by digital interactions, developing healthy social media habits is crucial for maintaining mental well-being and fostering meaningful connections. The pervasive nature of social media can lead to excessive use, which is often associated with various negative outcomes such as stress, anxiety, and decreased productivity. Understanding and implementing strategies to cultivate healthy social media habits can help mitigate these risks, enhancing the benefits of digital connectivity while reducing potential harms.

Understanding the Impact of Social Media

The first step in developing healthy habits is understanding the profound impact social media can have on mental health and daily life. Research has consistently linked excessive social media use with feelings of inadequacy, depression, and heightened anxiety. The mechanisms behind these effects often include negative social comparison, disruption of sleep patterns, and a sense of "time wasted" that could have been used for more fulfilling activities. Recognizing these potential pitfalls is essential for taking proactive steps toward healthier usage.

Setting Clear Goals and Intentions

Users should set clear goals and intentions for their social media use. This involves asking fundamental questions about why they are using these platforms and what they hope to gain from them. Whether it's staying in touch with family, networking for career opportunities, or accessing educational content, having specific objectives can help users stay focused and avoid aimless browsing, which often leads to overuse.

Creating a Balanced Online-Offline Life

Maintaining a balance between online activities and offline life is critical. Social media should not replace face-to-face interactions but rather complement them. To foster this balance, users can:

Schedule specific times for social media use and stick to these schedules.

Make time for offline activities that enrich their lives, such as hobbies, exercise, or spending time in nature.

Use social media to enhance real-world relationships, for example, by sharing information or coordinating events, rather than letting it replace these interactions.

Utilizing Tools for Managing Use

Most social media platforms and smartphones now offer tools to help manage usage. These can include:

Screen time trackers that provide insights into how much time is spent on various apps.

Features that allow users to set limits on their usage or schedule downtime.

Notifications settings that can be adjusted to reduce the frequency of alerts, which often trigger the impulse to check devices.

Engaging with Content Consciously

Consuming content passively on social media can lead to negative experiences, such as envy or resentment. Engaging with content more consciously involves:

Choosing to follow accounts that inspire and uplift rather than induce negativity or feelings of inadequacy.

Interacting actively by leaving thoughtful comments or sharing content that aligns with personal values, which can lead to more meaningful exchanges and a sense of community.

Critical Consumption of Information

Developing critical thinking skills is essential for navigating the vast amounts of information on social media. This includes:

Verifying the credibility of information before sharing it.

Being aware of biases in the content encountered.

Educating oneself on recognizing fake news and misinformation.

Practicing Digital Detoxes

Regular digital detoxes can help mitigate the risk of addiction and provide space for reflection on the role of digital media in one's life. This might involve:

Designating one day a week as a social media-free day.

Taking extended breaks during vacations or at least reducing usage during these times.

Seeking Professional Help When Necessary

If social media use becomes problematic, it may be necessary to seek professional help. Signs that professional guidance might be needed include:

Feeling anxious or stressed about not being able to access social media.

Notable impacts on personal or professional relationships due to social media use.

Significant disturbance in sleep patterns or daily routines.

• 153 •

Developing healthy social media habits is crucial for leveraging the benefits of these platforms without falling prey to their potential downsides. By understanding the impacts of social media, setting clear usage intentions, maintaining a balanced online-offline life, and utilizing available tools, individuals can enjoy a healthier, more controlled digital life. These habits not only enhance personal well-being but also contribute to a more positive and productive social media environment.

"The accessibility of vast networks through social media offers adolescents the unique opportunity to influence and be influenced by global peers. This interconnectedness, while empowering, also exposes them to cyberbullying and peer pressure on an international scale. Educating them about safe online practices and the importance of kindness and respect in digital interactions is crucial. We have the opportunity to foster a generation that uses its global reach for positive influence. Let's instill in them the values of empathy and integrity, making the digital world a better place."

ᐅᐅᐅ

THIRTY-FIVE

Social Media Detox: Benefits and Challenges

In today's hyperconnected world, social media has become a ubiquitous presence in daily life, offering myriad benefits from increased connectivity to instant information access. However, excessive engagement with social media can lead to negative psychological impacts, including stress, anxiety, and a decrease in personal well-being. Recognizing these potential pitfalls, many are turning to the concept of a social media detox—a conscious decision to step back from social media use temporarily to rebalance and refocus one's life. This essay explores the benefits and challenges of undergoing a social media detox, providing insight into why it might be necessary and how it can be effectively implemented.

Benefits of a Social Media Detox

Improved Mental Health One of the most significant benefits of a social media detox is the potential improvement in mental health. Regular use of social media can lead to increased feelings of inadequacy and anxiety, largely due to constant comparisons with the seemingly perfect lives of others and the pressure to curate a favorable online presence. A detox can mitigate these feelings by reducing exposure to stress-inducing content, thereby potentially alleviating symptoms of depression and anxiety.

Enhanced Productivity Social media can be a profound distraction due to its dynamic and interactive nature. Regular notifications and the allure of new content can disrupt focus and decrease productivity. By taking a break from social media, individuals often experience fewer interruptions and are able to redirect their attention to more productive tasks, leading to better time management and higher efficiency in both personal and professional endeavors.

Increased Real-World Interactions A social media detox can lead to more time spent in face-to-face interactions, which are crucial for building stronger interpersonal relationships. Physical interactions have a richness and depth that social media cannot replicate. Re-engaging with the world away from digital screens can help deepen connections with friends and family, fostering a sense of community and belonging.

Reclaimed Personal Time Time spent scrolling through social media is often passive and unfulfilling. By detoxing, individuals reclaim this time, allowing for engagement in activities that contribute to personal growth and happiness. This could include pursuing hobbies, reading, exercising, or simply taking time to relax and reflect.

Better Sleep Patterns The use of social media, especially before bedtime, can significantly impair sleep quality. The blue light emitted by screens suppresses melatonin production, while the engaging content keeps the mind active, making it harder to fall asleep. A detox from social media, particularly in the evening hours, can lead to improved sleep patterns and higher quality sleep.

Challenges of a Social Media Detox

Fear of Missing Out (FOMO) One of the primary challenges faced during a social media detox is the pervasive fear of missing out. Social media platforms are key venues for sharing news and events, and stepping away can lead to anxiety about being out of the loop on personal news or global events. This can make sticking to a detox challenging, as the urge to check updates can be compelling.

Social Isolation For many, social media is a major tool for staying connected, especially for those with friends and family who are geographically distant. A detox might lead to feelings of isolation and disconnection from one's social circle, which can be particularly challenging for individuals who rely on digital platforms for most of their social interactions.

Adjustment Period The integration of social media into daily routines means that removing it can lead to an adjustment period where one might struggle to find ways to fill the time previously spent on these platforms. This can be uncomfortable and may deter individuals from continuing their detox.

Work-Related Challenges For professionals who use social media as part of their job, a detox is not simply a personal choice but one that can have professional ramifications. Finding the balance between a necessary detox for personal well-being and maintaining a professional online presence can be difficult.

Implementing a Successful Social Media Detox

Successfully implementing a social media detox requires planning and commitment. It can be helpful to set clear goals and a specific time frame for the detox, whether it be a few days, weeks, or even months. Communicating these intentions to friends and family can also provide support and accountability. Additionally, finding alternative activities to fill the time usually spent on social media can ease the transition and help solidify new, healthier habits.

While a social media detox presents certain challenges, the benefits can be profound, leading to improved mental health, productivity, and personal relationships. As digital platforms continue to evolve, taking regular breaks from social media may become an essential strategy for maintaining balance and ensuring that technology serves to enhance rather than detract from overall well-being.

ԲԲԲ

THIRTY-SIX

PROFESSIONAL PERSPECTIVES: PSYCHOLOGISTS AND EDUCATORS ON SOCIAL MEDIA

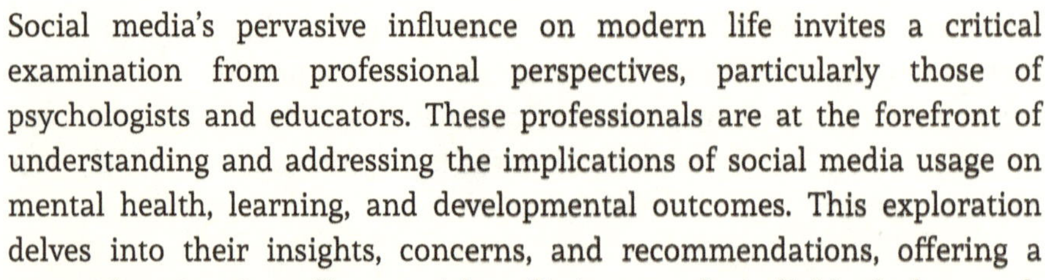

Social media's pervasive influence on modern life invites a critical examination from professional perspectives, particularly those of psychologists and educators. These professionals are at the forefront of understanding and addressing the implications of social media usage on mental health, learning, and developmental outcomes. This exploration delves into their insights, concerns, and recommendations, offering a comprehensive view of how social media impacts the individuals they work with daily.

Psychologists: Understanding the Mental Health Implications

Psychologists have raised significant concerns about the impact of social media on mental health, highlighting several key areas where these platforms can affect well-being.

Addiction and Compulsive Behavior Psychologists note that social media can exhibit addictive qualities, particularly among adolescents and young adults. The intermittent reinforcements provided by likes, comments, and shares act similarly to gambling rewards, encouraging constant checking and interaction. This compulsive behavior can lead to significant distress, affecting sleep, productivity, and face-to-face relationships.

Anxiety and Depression The link between social media usage and increased levels of anxiety and depression is a major concern for psychologists. They point out that constant social comparison, fear of missing out (FOMO), and the pressure to maintain an idealized online persona can exacerbate feelings of inadequacy and anxiety. Moreover, exposure to cyberbullying and online harassment has been directly associated with depressive symptoms, especially in younger users.

Self-Esteem and Body Image Psychologists are particularly worried about the impact of social media on self-esteem and body image. Platforms like Instagram, which heavily emphasize visual content, can lead to negative body image and low self-esteem as users compare themselves to often unattainable standards of beauty and success. These issues are particularly acute among teenagers and young women, who are highly represented on these platforms.

Recommendations To mitigate these risks, psychologists recommend setting boundaries around social media use, such as designated unplugged times or no-device zones in homes. They also emphasize the importance of fostering real-world relationships and activities that do not involve screens. For those struggling with mental health issues related to social media, psychologists advocate for professional counseling and, if necessary, participating in social media detox programs.

Educators: Social Media's Impact on Learning and Development

Educators discuss the dual nature of social media's impact on learning environments and student development. While acknowledging the benefits, they also express concerns about the potential distractions and negative effects on students' ability to concentrate and engage deeply with academic material.

Enhancing Learning On the positive side, educators note that social media can be a powerful tool for enhancing educational outcomes. Platforms can facilitate collaboration among students, allow for instant access to educational content and experts worldwide, and enable learning through digital and interactive formats that engage students more effectively than traditional methods.

Distraction and Attention Issues However, educators frequently cite the distracting nature of social media as a significant detriment to learning. The constant notifications and the allure of always-accessible entertainment can undermine students' attention spans and reduce their ability to engage in sustained, deep learning. This is seen in classrooms where students multitask between educational tasks and social media, often leading to reduced comprehension and retention of material.

Cyberbullying and School Environment Another concern is the extension of bullying into the digital realm. Cyberbullying can have a profound effect on students' emotional well-being and school performance. Educators stress the need for schools to implement policies that address cyberbullying and educate students about digital citizenship.

Recommendations Educators recommend integrating social media literacy into the school curriculum to teach students how to use these platforms responsibly and effectively. They also suggest using technology like educational apps and platforms that can harness the educational benefits of digital engagement without the negative aspects of traditional social media sites.

The perspectives of psychologists and educators provide vital insights into the complex effects of social media on individuals and society. By understanding these professional viewpoints, stakeholders—including parents, policymakers, and the users themselves—can develop strategies to leverage the benefits of social media while mitigating its risks. This balanced approach is essential for ensuring that social media contributes positively to mental health and educational outcomes.

ᏫᏫᏫ

"As adolescents navigate the virtual corridors of social media, the line between private and public personas can become dangerously thin. Educating them on the importance of maintaining privacy online protects more than just their personal information—it safeguards their autonomy. We must teach them that privacy settings are not just digital tools but are essential to personal security and self-respect. Encouraging them to manage their online presence wisely helps preserve their freedom to express themselves within safe boundaries. Let's empower them with knowledge and tools to protect their digital selves."

ppp

THIRTY-SEVEN

Global Initiatives to Combat Social Media Risks

As the impact of social media on society becomes increasingly apparent, global initiatives aimed at mitigating its risks have begun to emerge. These initiatives involve a wide array of stakeholders, including governments, international organizations, social media companies, non-profits, and community groups, each bringing different perspectives and solutions to the table. Understanding these efforts provides insight into the collective approach being taken to address the challenges posed by social media, from misinformation and cyberbullying to privacy breaches and mental health concerns.

International Regulations and Policy Frameworks

One of the primary strategies for addressing social media risks involves the implementation of regulatory frameworks by governments and international bodies. These regulations are designed to ensure that social media platforms operate responsibly, protect users, and contribute positively to society.

European Union: General Data Protection Regulation (GDPR) The GDPR, which came into effect in May 2018, has set a global standard for data protection and privacy. Its stringent requirements on data consent, user rights to access and erase their data, and hefty fines for violations have forced social media companies to significantly alter their operations worldwide. GDPR has spurred similar legislative initiatives in other regions, emphasizing user privacy and data security.

Australia: eSafety Commissioner Australia has established an eSafety Commissioner, the world's first government regulatory agency committed to keeping citizens safer online. The Commissioner's office has a wide range of powers, from addressing cyberbullying among children to tackling image-based abuse and online extremism. This model represents a proactive and comprehensive national approach to digital safety, offering a template for other countries.

NetzDG Law in Germany Germany's Network Enforcement Act, commonly known as NetzDG, compels social media platforms to remove illegal content, including hate speech and defamation, within strict timelines or face substantial fines. This law highlights the country's aggressive stance on curbing harmful online speech and sets a precedent for other nations considering similar regulations.

Global Coalitions and Partnerships

Recognizing that social media challenges cross national boundaries, various global coalitions and partnerships have been formed to address these issues collectively.

The Global Internet Forum to Counter Terrorism (GIFCT) Founded by major tech companies like Facebook, Microsoft, Twitter, and YouTube, GIFCT aims to prevent terrorists and violent extremists from exploiting digital platforms. The initiative focuses on technological solutions, knowledge sharing, and research to combat extremist content online.

Partnership on AI The Partnership on AI involves stakeholders from academia, civil society, and industry collaborating to study and formulate best practices on AI technologies, including those that underpin social media platforms. The partnership's goal is to ensure that AI applications, including content moderation algorithms, are developed and implemented responsibly and ethically.

Educational Programs and Public Awareness Campaigns

Alongside regulatory and partnership efforts, educational programs and public awareness campaigns play a crucial role in combating social media risks by empowering users to navigate digital spaces more safely.

Media Literacy Initiatives UNESCO, among other international organizations, has championed media literacy to help individuals develop critical thinking skills necessary to navigate the complex media landscape, including social media. These programs teach users to identify misinformation, understand media biases, and engage with content critically.

Digital Citizenship Education Programs aimed at fostering digital citizenship educate users about their rights and responsibilities online. These initiatives promote a safe and responsible use of the internet, emphasizing respect, privacy, and the importance of contributing positively to online communities.

Technological Solutions and Innovations

Efforts to leverage technology in order to reduce social media risks are also gaining traction. Innovations include advanced AI-driven content moderation systems that can detect and act on harmful content more effectively and privacy-enhancing technologies that protect user data from unauthorized access and breaches.

The global initiatives to combat social media risks are diverse and multifaceted, reflecting the complex nature of the challenges posed by digital platforms. By integrating regulatory frameworks, international partnerships, educational efforts, and technological innovations, these initiatives aim to create safer online environments. As social media continues to evolve, ongoing collaboration and adaptation will be essential to address emerging risks and ensure that social media can be a force for good in the global community.

ppp

THIRTY-EIGHT

Technology and Human Connection: Finding Balance

In the digital age, technology, particularly social media, has significantly altered how we connect and interact with each other. While these platforms offer unprecedented opportunities for staying connected, they also present challenges to authentic human interactions. Finding a balance between technology use and maintaining meaningful human connections is essential for personal well-being and societal health. This essay explores the dual impact of technology on human connection and discusses strategies for achieving a harmonious balance.

The Impact of Technology on Human Connections

Technology's influence on human relationships can be seen in both positive and negative lights, significantly affecting how relationships are formed, maintained, and sometimes ended.

Enhanced Connectivity Technology, especially social media, has the profound ability to connect people across geographical boundaries. It enables friends and families to stay in touch despite physical distances, supports the formation of online communities based on shared interests, and facilitates professional networking that was not possible before. This connectivity can be particularly vital in times of crisis, such as during natural disasters or global pandemics, where traditional communication channels might be disrupted.

Altered Communication Patterns While technology allows for constant connectivity, it also changes the nature of our interactions. Digital communication often lacks the nuances of face-to-face conversations, such as body language, tone, and immediate emotional responses, which are crucial for building deep and meaningful relationships. Overreliance on text-based communication can lead to misunderstandings and a sense of emotional distance, even in close relationships.

Distraction and Fragmentation The constant notifications and the allure of ever-refreshing content can lead to fragmented attention during physical interactions. The phenomenon of "phubbing," where people snub their companions in favor of their smartphones, is a clear example of how technology can interfere with real-world connections, leading to feelings of neglect and dissatisfaction in relationships.

Depersonalization and Surface-Level Relationships Social media platforms often encourage a culture of surface-level interactions, where the number of likes, comments, and shares becomes a measure of social success. These interactions, while gratifying, are rarely as fulfilling as deeper personal connections and can lead to a depersonalization of relationships, where connections are maintained passively through digital interactions rather than active, personal engagement.

Strategies for Balancing Technology and Human Connection

Achieving a balance between leveraging the benefits of technology and maintaining genuine human connections involves intentional actions and mindful usage of digital tools.

Mindful Technology Use Being mindful about how and when to use technology can help mitigate its intrusive aspects. This might involve setting specific times for checking social media, turning off non-essential notifications, or designating tech-free zones and times, such as during meals or family gatherings, to ensure quality time with loved ones.

Prioritizing Face-to-Face Interactions Prioritizing in-person interactions when possible can help maintain the depth and quality of relationships. Engaging in shared activities, such as hobbies, sports, or community service, can strengthen bonds and improve well-being far more than virtual interactions.

Using Technology to Enhance Rather Than Replace Interactions Technology should be used to enhance relationships rather than replace them. For instance, video calls can be a wonderful way to stay in touch with distant relatives, offering more personal interaction than text messages or emails. Similarly, social media can be used strategically to arrange in-person gatherings or to share meaningful content that sparks real conversations.

Educational Programs on Digital Literacy Educational programs that teach digital literacy, including the healthy use of technology, are crucial. These programs can help individuals understand the impact of digital tools on mental health and relationships and provide strategies for managing their digital consumption.

Therapeutic Interventions For those struggling to balance technology with personal relationships, therapeutic interventions can be beneficial. Counseling or therapy can offer strategies to address issues like internet addiction, social anxiety facilitated by digital interactions, or conflicts in relationships due to technology use.

Finding a balance between technology use and human connections is critical in the digital age. While technology provides valuable tools for enhancing connectivity, it also poses risks to the quality of our human interactions. By adopting mindful usage practices, prioritizing face-to-face engagements, and utilizing educational resources, individuals can enjoy the benefits of technology without compromising the depth of their human connections. As society continues to evolve with technological advances, fostering awareness and intentional behavior regarding our digital habits will be key to maintaining this balance.

ppp

"The role of influencers in social media can shape the aspirations and ideologies of adolescents, often placing them on pedestals that skew realistic ambitions. It is important to discuss the curated nature of such online lives and the business dynamics behind them. Encouraging critical thinking about the content they consume helps them understand the distinction between being influenced and being informed. By fostering media literacy, we enable them to make informed choices about who they admire and why. Let's guide them to aspire to achievements that are grounded in reality, not just in visibility."

ᐅᐅᐅ

THIRTY-NINE
CONCLUSIONS AND RECOMMENDATIONS

In exploring the multifaceted realm of social media and its profound impact on society, several key conclusions emerge, alongside strategic recommendations aimed at maximizing the benefits while mitigating the risks associated with digital life. These insights are crucial for policymakers, educators, health professionals, parents, and users themselves, as they navigate the complexities of an increasingly digital world.

Pervasiveness and Impact Social media is not just a platform for social interaction but a significant influence on cultural, political, and personal dimensions of life. Its ability to shape public opinion, influence market trends, and alter communication dynamics underscores its role as a powerful tool in modern society.

Benefits and Opportunities Social media offers numerous benefits, including enhanced connectivity, opportunities for educational engagement, platforms for business and entrepreneurship, and avenues for political and social activism. These platforms have democratized information, giving a voice to the marginalized and offering new ways to learn, connect, and engage.

Risks and Challenges Despite its benefits, social media also poses significant risks such as privacy concerns, misinformation, cyberbullying, and the potential for addiction. These issues can have severe implications for mental health, social cohesion, and democratic processes.

Need for Balanced Engagement The dual nature of social media necessitates a balanced approach to its use. Users need to be mindful of their digital consumption to protect their mental health and maintain quality interpersonal relationships.

Recommendations

Enhancing Digital Literacy

For Individuals: Users of all ages should be educated about the functionalities, benefits, and risks of social media. This education should include how to maintain privacy settings, recognize misinformation, and understand the impact of digital footprints.

For Educational Institutions: Schools and universities should integrate digital literacy into their curricula to prepare students for a digital world, focusing on critical thinking, ethical online behavior, and the safe use of technology.

Regulatory and Policy Frameworks

Governments and regulatory bodies should develop and enforce regulations that protect users from online harms while supporting freedom of expression. These regulations should address data privacy, age-appropriate content, cyberbullying, and the responsibilities of social media platforms to moderate content and protect user rights.

International cooperation is essential to address the global nature of digital platforms and ensure that regulatory measures are effective across borders.

Promoting Mental Health and Well-being

Mental health professionals and organizations should create resources and programs that address the psychological impacts of social media use. These should include strategies for managing online stressors and promoting a healthy digital-life balance.

Workplaces and educational institutions should provide support systems and workshops that encourage healthy social media habits and offer guidance on managing digital stress.

Technological Innovations

Technology developers and social media platforms should continue to innovate in ways that enhance user safety and data security. Advancements in artificial intelligence, for instance, can improve content moderation and help detect harmful behavior.

Platforms should be transparent about their algorithms and data practices to build trust and empower users.

Community and Parental Engagement

Parents must play an active role in guiding their children's social media use by setting good examples, discussing online risks, and encouraging healthy habits.

Communities should foster environments where digital wellness is promoted through public campaigns, workshops, and resources that highlight the importance of balancing online and offline life.

As we advance further into the digital age, the need for a comprehensive and nuanced understanding of social media becomes increasingly imperative. By adopting the recommendations outlined, stakeholders across various sectors can help ensure that social media serves as a tool for positive change and personal growth rather than a source of risk. Ultimately, the goal is to cultivate a digital landscape where safety, privacy, and meaningful connectivity are not just ideals, but realities for all users.

ಶಿಶಿಶಿ

"The rapid pace of social media can make life feel like a series of fast-forward moments, where slow reflection seems a thing of the past. Encouraging adolescents to take time to reflect on their experiences allows them to process their lives more deeply. This practice can enrich their understanding of themselves and their relationships, beyond the immediate reactions that social media often demands. Teaching them the value of contemplation amidst constant connectivity can lead to more profound personal growth. Let's help them discover the power of pausing and reflecting, fostering a deeper engagement with the world both online and off."

ᐅᐅᐅ

FORTY

BIBLIOGRAPHY

Bayer, J. B., Ellison, N. B., Schoenebeck, S. Y., & Falk, E. B. (2016). Sharing the small moments: Ephemeral social interaction on Snapchat. *Information, Communication & Society, 19*(7), 956-977.

boyd, d. (2014). *It's complicated: The social lives of networked teens.* Yale University Press.

Ellison, N. B., Steinfield, C., & Lampe, C. (2007). The benefits of Facebook "friends:" Social capital and college students' use of online social network sites. *Journal of Computer-Mediated Communication, 12*(4), 1143-1168.

Festinger, L. (1954). A theory of social comparison processes. *Human Relations, 7*(2), 117-140.

Kross, E., Verduyn, P., Demiralp, E., Park, J., Lee, D. S., Lin, N., Shablack, H., Jonides, J., & Ybarra, O. (2013). Facebook use predicts declines in subjective well-being in young adults. *PLOS ONE, 8*(8), e69841.

Putnam, R. D. (2000). *Bowling Alone: The collapse and revival of American community.* Simon and Schuster.

Rosenberg, M. (1965). *Society and the adolescent self-image.* Princeton University Press.

Steinfield, C., Ellison, N. B., & Lampe, C. (2008). Social capital, self-esteem, and use of online social network sites: A longitudinal analysis. *Journal of*

Applied Developmental Psychology, 29(6), 434-445.

Twenge, J. M., Joiner, T. E., Rogers, M. L., & Martin, G. N. (2018). Increases in depressive symptoms, suicide-related outcomes, and suicide rates among U.S. adolescents after 2010 and links to increased new media screen time. *Clinical Psychological Science, 6*(1), 3-17.

Valkenburg, P. M., Peter, J., & Schouten, A. P. (2006). Friend networking sites and their relationship to adolescents' well-being and social self-esteem. *CyberPsychology & Behavior, 9*(5), 584-590.

Vogel, E. A., Rose, J. P., Roberts, L. R., & Eckles, K. (2014). Social comparison, social media, and self-esteem. *Psychology of Popular Media Culture, 3*(4), 206-222.

ውውው

Citation And References

This book represents the culmination of extensive research and meticulous analysis, incorporating a diverse range of sources, including numerous books, scholarly studies, and personal experiences. Additionally, I have scoured various websites to gather relevant information and data essential for the compilation of this work. I have taken every precaution to ensure the accuracy of the information presented and have diligently cited all sources to acknowledge their contributions.

Despite these efforts, the possibility of inadvertent errors remains. I deeply value the insights of my readers and appreciate any feedback that can help identify and rectify such inaccuracies. I encourage you to bring any discrepancies to my attention.

Your feedback is not only welcome but crucial, as it will aid in correcting current editions and enhancing the content of future ones. I am committed to maintaining the highest standards of accuracy and reliability in my work and thank you for your support and understanding.

Additionally, I firmly uphold the principle of freedom of speech and expression as guaranteed under Article 19(1)(a) of the Constitution of India, and I respect the diverse viewpoints and expressions of all readers.

ᖰᖰᖰ

Other Books Of The Author

1. Empowering Minds: A Journey into Women's Self-Discovery and Power
2. The Dynamics of Motivation: Catalyzing Thought into Action
3. Meditation and Mental Well Being: The Path to Inner Peace and Clarity
4. The Psychology of Child Education: Nurturing Future Generations
5. Ethical Enlightenment: A Modern Guide to Living with Integrity
6. Voices of Empowerment: Stories of Women Rising Against Odds
7. Social Psychology in Everyday Life: Understanding Human Connections
8. The Essence of Motivational Speaking: Inspiring Change in Others
9. Balancing Acts: Women, Work, and the Will to Lead
10. Guiding with Grace: Raising Children with Compassion and Awareness
11. The Power of Positive Aging: Embracing Life After Fifty
12. Building Resilient Communities: Social Work in Action
13. The Ethical Educator: Principles for Teaching and Learning
14. From Insight to Impact: Social Psychology for a Better World
15. The Ethics of Empathy: A Guide to Ethical Living
16. The Science of Empowering the Self: Navigating Life's Challenges with Psychological Wisdom
17. The Mindful Conscious Leader: Meditation Techniques for Modern Management
18. Pioneering Spirit: Women's Pathways to Leadership and Empowerment
19. Feeling to Healing: The Role of Emotional Intelligence in Child Development
20. Transformative Talks and Words of Inspiration: Insights into Motivational Oratory
21. Green Ethics: A Path to Sustainable Living
22. Spiritual Integrity: Navigating Life with Moral Compassion
23. Clean Living, Clean Society: The Ethics of Cleanliness
24. Patriotic Spirits: Building a Nation on Positive Attitudes
25. Innovative Integrity & Vibrant Visions: The Ethical and Entrepreneurial Spirit of Gujarat
26. Youthful Visions, Endless Possibilities: Inspiring Ethics and Motivation in Children
27. Living Your Legacy: How to Motivate Others by Living Your Values
28. Secret of Healing Conversations: Ethical Practices in Counselling and

ᐅᐅᐅ

Contact

Dr. Minakshi Bansal
Social Activist
Ahmedabad, Gujarat, Bharat
minakshiindiag20@yahoo.com

❦❦❦

|| LOKAHA SAMASTHAHA SUKHINO BHAVANTU ||